T0384918

An Analysis of

Georges Lefebvre's

The Coming of the French Revolution

Tom Stammers

Published by Macat International Ltd
24:13 Coda Centre, 189 Munster Road, London SW6 6AW.

Distributed exclusively by Routledge
2 Park Square, Milton Park, Abingdon, Oxon OX14 4RN
711 Third Avenue, New York, NY 10017, USA

Routledge is an imprint of the Taylor & Francis Group, an informa business

Copyright © 2017 by Macat International Ltd
Macat International has asserted its right under the Copyright, Designs and Patents Act
1988 to be identified as the copyright holder of this work.

www.macat.com
info@macat.com

Cataloguing in Publication Data
A catalogue record for this book is available from the British Library.
Library of Congress Cataloguing-in-Publication Data is available upon request.
Cover illustration: Etienne Gilfillan

ISBN 978-1-912302-71-0 (hardback)
ISBN 978-1-912128-19-8 (paperback)
ISBN 978-1-912281-59-6 (e-book)

Notice

CONTENTS

WAYS IN TO THE TEXT

Who Was Georges Lefebvre?   9
What Does *The Coming of the French Revolution* Say?   11
Why Does *The Coming of the French Revolution* Matter?   12

SECTION 1: INFLUENCES

Module 1: The Author and the Historical Context   16
Module 2: Academic Context   21
Module 3: The Problem   26
Module 4: The Author's Contribution   31

SECTION 2: IDEAS

Module 5: Main Ideas   37
Module 6: Secondary Ideas   42
Module 7: Achievement   47
Module 8: Place in the Author's Work   52

SECTION 3: IMPACT

Module 9: The First Responses   58
Module 10: The Evolving Debate   63
Module 11: Impact and Influence Today   69
Module 12: Where Next?   75

Glossary of Terms   81
People Mentioned in the Text   93
Works Cited   104

THE MACAT LIBRARY

The Macat Library is a series of unique academic explorations of seminal works in the humanities and social sciences – books and papers that have had a significant and widely recognised impact on their disciplines. It has been created to serve as much more than just a summary of what lies between the covers of a great book. It illuminates and explores the influences on, ideas of, and impact of that book. Our goal is to offer a learning resource that encourages critical thinking and fosters a better, deeper understanding of important ideas.

Each publication is divided into three Sections: Influences, Ideas, and Impact. Each Section has four Modules. These explore every important facet of the work, and the responses to it.

This Section-Module structure makes a Macat Library book easy to use, but it has another important feature. Because each Macat book is written to the same format, it is possible (and encouraged!) to cross-reference multiple Macat books along the same lines of inquiry or research. This allows the reader to open up interesting interdisciplinary pathways.

To further aid your reading, lists of glossary terms and people mentioned are included at the end of this book (these are indicated by an asterisk [*] throughout) – as well as a list of works cited.

Macat has worked with the University of Cambridge to identify the elements of critical thinking and understand the ways in which six different skills combine to enable effective thinking.
Three allow us to fully understand a problem; three more give us the tools to solve it. Together, these six skills make up the **PACIER** model of critical thinking. They are:

ANALYSIS – understanding how an argument is built
EVALUATION – exploring the strengths and weaknesses of an argument
INTERPRETATION – understanding issues of meaning

CREATIVE THINKING – coming up with new ideas and fresh connections
PROBLEM-SOLVING – producing strong solutions
REASONING – creating strong arguments

To find out more, visit **WWW.MACAT.COM.**

CRITICAL THINKING AND *THE COMING OF THE FRENCH REVOLUTION*

Primary critical thinking skill: EVALUATION
Secondary critical thinking skill: ANALYSIS

Georges Lefebvre was one of the most highly-regarded historians of the 20th century – and a key reason for the high reputation he enjoys can be found in *The Coming of the French Revolution*. Lefebvre's key contribution to the debate over what remains arguably one of history's most contentious and significant events in history was to deploy the critical thinking skill of evaluation to reveal weaknesses in existing arguments about the causes of the Revolution, and analytical skills to expose hidden assumptions in them. Rather than seeing events as driven by the aristocracy and the bourgeoisie – which then lost power to the urban workers – as was usual at the time, Lefebvre deployed years of research in regional archives to argue that the Revolution had had a fourth pillar: the peasantry.

Painting the upheaval as complex and multi-layered – while still privileging a predominantly economic interpretation – Lefebvre provides a compelling new narrative to explain why the French monarchy collapsed so suddenly in 1789: one that stressed the significance of a 'popular revolution' in the rural countryside.

ABOUT THE AUTHOR OF THE ORIGINAL WORK

Born in 1874, **Georges Lefebvre** grew up in the industrial French town of Lille, the son of an office worker. Beginning from these humble beginnings, Lefebvre reached the age of 50 before completing his dissertation on the peasantry of the French Revolution. Yet the 1930s and 1940s saw him write a series of experimental and definitive works of social history. At the time of his death in 1959, he had been hailed as one of the greatest authorities on 1789, and was widely seen as a guardian of the French republican tradition.

ABOUT THE AUTHOR OF THE ANALYSIS

Dr Thomas Stammers is lecturer in Modern European history at Durham University, where he specialises in the cultural history of France in the age of revolution. He is the author of *Collection, Recollection, Revolution: Scavenging the Past in Nineteenth-Century Paris.*
Dr Stammers's research interests include a wide range of historiographical and theoretical controversies related to eighteenth and nineteenth-century Europe.

ABOUT MACAT

GREAT WORKS FOR CRITICAL THINKING

Macat is focused on making the ideas of the world's great thinkers accessible and comprehensible to everybody, everywhere, in ways that promote the development of enhanced critical thinking skills.

It works with leading academics from the world's top universities to produce new analyses that focus on the ideas and the impact of the most influential works ever written across a wide variety of academic disciplines. Each of the works that sit at the heart of its growing library is an enduring example of great thinking. But by setting them in context – and looking at the influences that shaped their authors, as well as the responses they provoked – Macat encourages readers to look at these classics and game-changers with fresh eyes. Readers learn to think, engage and challenge their ideas, rather than simply accepting them.

'Macat offers an amazing first-of-its-kind tool for interdisciplinary learning and research. Its focus on works that transformed their disciplines and its rigorous approach, drawing on the world's leading experts and educational institutions, opens up a world-class education to anyone.'

Andreas Schleicher
Director for Education and Skills, Organisation for Economic
Co-operation and Development

'Macat is taking on some of the major challenges in university education … They have drawn together a strong team of active academics who are producing teaching materials that are novel in the breadth of their approach.'

Prof Lord Broers,
former Vice-Chancellor of the University of Cambridge

'The Macat vision is exceptionally exciting. It focuses upon new modes of learning which analyse and explain seminal texts which have profoundly influenced world thinking and so social and economic development. It promotes the kind of critical thinking which is essential for any society and economy.
This is the learning of the future.'

Rt Hon Charles Clarke, former UK Secretary of State for Education

'The Macat analyses provide immediate access to the critical conversation surrounding the books that have shaped their respective discipline, which will make them an invaluable resource to all of those, students and teachers, working in the field.'

Professor William Tronzo, University of California at San Diego

WAYS IN TO THE TEXT

KEY POINTS

- In the first half of the twentieth century, the French historian Georges Lefebvre was considered the leading historian of the French Revolution*—a period of political upheaval that began in 1789, in the course of which the French monarchy* was overthrown and great political reforms were instituted. Lefebvre's explanation of why the revolution happened set the boundaries for all the debate that followed.

- Lefebvre's book identified and analyzed the four fronts on which the French monarchy's authority collapsed in the course of 1789.

- Lefebvre was influential in portraying the revolution both as a vast social transformation and as a political crisis.

Who Was Georges Lefebvre?

Georges Lefebvre, the author of *The Coming of the French Revolution* (1939), was born in 1874 in Lille, France. His father, an office worker, did not earn enough to pay for his son's education; it was only through winning scholarships that he was able to stay at school and study at the University of Lille.

Lefebvre's road to recognition as a historian was long. Because he had not attended one of the prestigious Paris schools or universities, he had to work as a teacher in provincial schools for 20 years and only received his doctorate when he was 50 years old; his dissertation, "The Peasants of the North during the French Revolution," demonstrated an exceptional knowledge of regional and rural documents. His deep reading in the archives later led many to consider him the greatest living French authority on the French Revolution.[1]

After being appointed to the University of Strasbourg, where he met the leaders of the *Annales** school of history (a deeply influential movement recognized for an approach to writing history that frequently emphasized the social context of the field of study), Lefebvre moved to France's most prestigious university, the Sorbonne,* in 1935. Two years later he was offered the position of Chair of the History of the French Revolution. In 1939, Lefebvre published *Quatre-Vingt Neuf* (translated into English as *The Coming of the French Revolution*), to mark the celebrations of the 150th anniversary of 1789. It presented a detailed analysis both of why the French Revolution had started, and of why it was a cause worth fighting for.

The book's message was very timely: in 1940, during World War II,* Nazi* Germany invaded France and overthrew the government. The brutal occupation that followed was very difficult for Lefebvre personally: his brother was killed fighting for the French Resistance,* and his teaching salary was stopped.[2]

When the war ended in 1945, Lefebvre was hailed as a symbol of resistance, both in France and in the wider world. English translations of his work soon followed and his international reputation soared. In the years before his death in 1959 he was an enormously important figure, and was hailed as a pioneer in the field of social history*[3]—a form of historical research that examines social structures and routinely considers the historical significance and experiences of people outside the social and political elite.

What Does *The Coming of the French Revolution* Say?

The Coming of the French Revolution, published in 1939, traces the reasons why the authority of the ruling French monarchy collapsed over the course of 1789. Focusing on the events of a single year, Lefebvre explains why royal power unraveled so quickly and unexpectedly. He broke his work into the analysis of four key social groups:

- the aristocracy* (the small, privileged, ruling class)
- the bourgeoisie* (roughly, the propertied urban middle class who made a living by trading and providing services)
- the urban crowds (workers living in the city)
- the peasantry (the traditional class of farmers and farm laborers).

He noted that each group had their own motives for refusing to accept royal authority, and there was little coordination between their actions. The situation developed from a revolt into a full revolution because of the way these four groups responded to events that no one had predicted.

Influenced by the theory proposed by the German economist and political philosopher Karl Marx* that capitalism* would be destroyed and replaced by a more equitable system, Lefebvre emphasized the role of class struggle* (the conflict between different social groups) in driving the French Revolution. The revolution's origins, he argues, went far back in time and were rooted in general conflicts in French society.

The group most able to impose their values in 1789 were the bourgeoisie, a class Lefebvre believed had been growing in wealth and power for centuries, and who had grown resentful of the aristocracy's attempts to block their advance. However, the bourgeoisie were only able to succeed in 1789 because of the "popular revolution" by ordinary people in the French towns and countryside. It took the collective action of urban and rural communities to make sure that the promises of reform made that year at the assembly known as the Estates General* were secured.

Thanks to the political upheavals of 1789, the power of the monarchy was dramatically reduced and new ideas of popular sovereignty*—the notion that it is the people who are the source of political authority—flourished. The revolution also led to the abolition both of inherited privileges and of the remnants of feudalism* (a medieval social system where landowners protected tenants in return for free labor). This was proclaimed in the August Decrees,* in which the aristocratic deputies*—representatives—in the National Assembly voted to give up many of their titles and privileges, mainly because they feared a peasant revolt.

The Coming of The French Revolution stood out because of its thorough research. Influenced by his colleagues in the *Annales* school, Lefebvre drew on different disciplines, including psychology and sociology, to shape his conclusions. He brought credibility to "history from below,"* the idea that events could be understood by what happened to ordinary people, not just those with power and influence. The American historian Robert R. Palmer* translated his book into English in 1947. Soon afterwards it became required reading at university campuses across the United Kingdom and the United States; its influence is still felt today. Scholars considering the social elements that contributed to the events of 1789 will, without doubt, turn to it at some point.

Why Does *The Coming of the French Revolution* Matter?

The Coming of the French Revolution asks a simple question: why did the strongest monarchy on the European continent collapse so dramatically in 1789? Lefebvre's work matters because it helps the reader to understand the social and economic issues that led to the revolution. It also pushes readers to think about the way ideas and psychology affect behavior. In that way, it underlines a number of motives, people, and pressures that came together in unexpected ways to bring about the revolution.

The book gives a clear description of the events of 1789. It helps readers understand how an event that had seemed unthinkable actually came to pass. It also provides a powerful account of what the French Revolution meant for contemporaries and later generations. Even today in France the attitude a person has towards the revolution defines many of their political beliefs. Lefebvre's book provides a classic socialist* account of why the revolution was a profound historical turning point, not only for France, but for all humanity.

It is important to note that Lefebvre's arguments had some weaknesses. The work was a product of its time, written under the influence of Marxist* ideas and with the aim of defending France's republican* political system on the brink of World War II. Later scholars who looked back at what had happened disagreed with the description Lefebvre gives of the four distinct social classes (the aristocracy, the bourgeoisie, the urban workers, and the peasants).

Lefebvre's work sparked a debate about continuity and change, suggesting that 1789 marked the start of the modern world by ending feudalism and bringing in capitalism (today, the dominant economic and social model in the Western world). Other scholars from the 1950s and 1960s said this was a simplistic view; capitalism was a force in French society *before* the revolution, they argued, and what was more, the nobility had already given up many of their powers before 1789.

According to the French historian François Furet,* the French Revolution mainly transformed how people thought about politics rather than transforming social structures.[4] The disputes between Lefebvre, his pupils, and his critics were heavily influenced by the Cold War* (a period when tensions ran high between the United States and the Soviet Union,* and the nations aligned to each country, between 1945 and 1991). Reading Lefebvre encourages the reader to think critically about the way long-term, medium-term, and short-term factors influence world events, and how historiography has developed against changing political contexts.

NOTES

1   Paul Beik, preface to Georges Lefebvre, *The French Revolution: From its Origins to 1793* (New York: Columbia University Press, 1962), ix–xv.

2   Claude Mazauric, "Les Chaussées sont désertes, plus de passants sur les chemins: La SER dans la tourmente: 1940–1945," *Annales historiques de la Révolution française* 353 (2008).

3   Beatrice Hyslop, "Georges Lefebvre, Historian," *French Historical Studies* 1 (1960), 265–82.

4   François Furet, *Interpreting the French Revolution* (Cambridge: Cambridge University Press, 1981).

SECTION 1
INFLUENCES

MODULE 1
THE AUTHOR AND THE HISTORICAL CONTEXT

KEY POINTS

- *The Coming of the French Revolution* offers a definitive vision of the causes of the French Revolution*—a period of radical social turmoil that began in 1879.

- Lefebvre was an innovative historian, digging through provincial archives and emphasizing the importance of overlooked social groups.

- He wrote to provide a broad vision of the revolution that could appeal to everyone at a time when the Third Republic*—France's government, founded on principles lain down in the years of the revolution—was threatened by the Nazi* invasion.

Why Read This Text?

George Lefebvre's *The Coming of the French Revolution* (1939) still provides the definitive explanation of the causes of the French Revolution. Although the revolution broke out in 1789, the social tensions between the nation's social classes that exploded that summer had been building up for many decades. Lefebvre identified four separate social groups as central to why the revolution came about when and how it did. It took all four groups doing something at the same time to smash the authority of the king and the power of the monarchy.*

The Coming of the French Revolution gives a balanced account of the factors that led to revolution. It mixes an analysis of the struggles in Paris and in Versailles,* where the palace of the French kings was

> ❝ Youth of 1939! The Declaration [of the Rights of Man]* is also a tradition, a glorious tradition. Listen, as you read it, to the voice of your forefathers, to those who shouted 'Long live the Nation!' as they fought at Valmy, Jemappes and at Fleurus.* They gave you a freedom, a noble right that, in all the universe, only mankind can enjoy. ❞
>
> Georges Lefebvre, *The Coming of the French Revolution*

situated, with the commotion in Paris and the brewing violence in the countryside. Lefebvre believed that the revolution had both social and economic causes—but he also explored the political and ideological issues that fed into the events of 1789. Scholars have pointed out omissions in Lefebvre's work; some of his ideas have been also challenged. However, up to now, no one has produced a narrative of 1789 whose clarity and coherence can be compared with *The Coming of the French Revolution*.

Author's Life

Georges Lefebvre was born in 1874 in the industrial city of Lille in France. His father was an office worker and his family belonged to the lower middle class. Lefebvre's father could not afford to pay for his son's education, which meant he needed to win scholarships in order to study at the University of Lille. These experiences were a factor in Lefebvre wanting to write a "history from below"*—according to which historians should try to recapture the experiences and viewpoints of ordinary people, not just the political and social elite. Lefebvre was profoundly shaped by socialist* politics, like his hero Jean Jaurès,* the leader of the French Socialist Party, who wanted to replace the economic system of capitalism* and its highly competitive structure with a new system based around social justice and the redistribution of wealth. For Lefebvre, the most important early attempt to create this fairer social order happened during the French Revolution of 1789.

Lefebvre's road to recognition as a historian was long. Because he had not attended one of the prestigious Paris schools or universities, he had to work as a teacher in provincial schools for 20 years, and only received his doctorate when he was 50 years old. Thanks to a much admired thesis on the French peasantry, Lefebvre joined the University of Strasbourg in 1927, where he became friendly with the *Annales** historians Lucien Febvre* and Marc Bloch.* The *Annales* school pioneered work in new ways of studying history, especially using ideas from other disciplines such as psychology, anthropology, and economics.

In 1937 he was made Chair of the History of the French Revolution at the Sorbonne,* the most prestigious university in France. He published *The Coming of the French Revolution* two years later, in 1939.

In 1940, however, Adolf Hitler's* Germany invaded France. France's new government, established in the city of Vichy,* collaborated with the Nazi invaders. Lefebvre kept up his teaching on the revolution in defiance of the German occupation; his brother was beheaded for his role in the French Resistance.* After the war, Lefebvre regained his authority as a major scholar and his works were translated into English, cementing his reputation in the United Kingdom and the United States. Before his death in 1959 he was considered the world's greatest living authority on the French Revolution.

Author's Background

Lefebvre wrote *The Coming of the French Revolution* in the 1930s, a decade of deep divisions in Europe between the political right* and the political left.* There were similar divides within France itself and most people's current political views could be understood by the way they described the legacy of the French Revolution. The revolution and its aftermath were viewed as a disaster by many on the right.[1] In this view, the old regime* that had existed before 1789, with a monarchy at its heart, had been swept away almost by short-sighted blunders. What had replaced it were abstract and vague philosophical ideas that could only cause confusion. In place of the monarchy, the revolutionaries established a dictatorship and the bloody Terror* of the years between 1792 and 1794, in the course of which political factionalism—disputes between different groups inside the new government and their supporters—led to many thousands of executions.

Not everyone on the left celebrated the revolution either. Socialists were convinced that the bourgeoisie* (the middle class, wealthy from the labor of the working class) had seized control of the revolution to advance their own interests. The communist* historian Albert Mathiez* argued that, aside from the brief government headed by Maximilien Robespierre* between 1793 and 1794, the revolution failed to deliver any meaningful social reforms for the ordinary people.[2] So opinion was split.

The threat posed by the extreme right-wing ideology of fascism,* however, both at home and abroad, brought together a Popular Front* government in 1936 under the socialist politician Léon Blum.* In this government, defenders of the moderate Third Republic*—which had existed in France since 1870 and which was committed to values inherited from the revolution—stood shoulder to shoulder with radical Marxists.*

Lefebvre wanted to write a history that could reconcile many of these differences of opinion. He believed in the Third Republic and wanted to defend it against its many critics on both the right and the left. One of his aims in *The Coming of The French Revolution* was to provide a vision of France that *all* French people could believe in.[3]

NOTES

1   Pierre Gaxotte, *La Révolution française* (Paris: Fayard,1928); Léon Daudet,
    Deux idoles sanguinaires: La Révolution et son fils Bonaparte (Paris: Albin
    Michel, 1939); Jacques Bainville, *Histoire de France* (Paris: Fayard, 1924).

2   Albert Mathiez, *The French Revolution* [1922–7], trans. C. A. Phillips (New
    York: Russell and Russell, 1962).

3   Jules Michelet, *Histoire de la Révolution française*, 7 vols. (Paris, 1847–53);
    Louis Blanc, *Histoire de la Révolution française*, 12 vols. (Paris, 1847–62);
    Alphonse Aulard, *Histoire politique de la Révolution française: Origines et de
    développement de la démocratie française* 1789–1804 (Paris, 1901).

MODULE 2
ACADEMIC CONTEXT

KEY POINTS

- Lefebvre believed that French society would benefit from a history of the French Revolution* of 1789 written from a left-wing perspective, offering a vision of the nation that all could believe in.

- He wrote in the tradition of his hero, the socialist leader Jean Jaurès,* whose explicitly socialist* history of the revolution depicted its events as the product of class struggle*—the tension between those who work and those who profit from that work.

- Lefebvre sought to build on this work by looking at the role of the French peasantry in the revolution.

The Work in its Context

Writing *The Coming of the French Revolution*, Georges Lefebvre was engaging with a tradition of preexisting literature on the French Revolution. Three strands of writing on the subject dominated the field at the start of the twentieth century:

- the republican* or Jacobin* tradition
- the conservative or counterrevolutionary* tradition
- the socialist or Marxist* tradition

Scholars in the Jacobin or republican tradition believed that the French Revolution was a victory for popular sovereignty* and popular justice—that is, the people themselves became the source of political authority. They celebrated 1789 as the dawn of liberty, when the nation threw off the shackles of an oppressive monarchy,* viewing the revolution as the work of the nation—or *le peuple*—as a whole. It

> ❝ Against the aristocracy* the peasants had far more substantial grievances than did the people of the cities, and it is natural therefore that they took it upon themselves to deal the blow by which the aristocracy was laid low. ❞
>
> Georges Lefebvre, *The Coming of the French Revolution*

symbolized an attempt to create a new kind of society that would defend the idea of freedom and equality for all.

In contrast, counterrevolutionary historians viewed the French Revolution as a catastrophe.[1] Starting with the cleric Abbé Augustin Barruel* in the 1790s, they believed it was the result of a conspiracy, plotted by individuals on the fringes of French society. According to them, these freethinkers,* Freemasons,* Protestants,* and foreigners led a gullible and bloodthirsty population astray. The revolution had tried to reshape French society in line with philosophical formulas that were not well thought out and that owed nothing to French tradition. The result, they argued, was disastrous.[2]

The third tradition derived from the German economist and political theorist Karl Marx,* who viewed 1789 as the result of class struggle. Although the revolution talked of ideas that should relate and apply to everyone, Marx suggested that it had, in fact, been the work of the bourgeoisie*—the propertied and professional classes. It was they who had swept away the old monarchy in order to create a society in which capitalism* could thrive.[3]

In his analysis, Lefebvre borrowed from the Jacobin and the Marxist traditions. Lefebvre believed that although 1789 had been a victory for the bourgeoisie, it nevertheless contained the seeds out of which a future socialism—the reforming of capitalism to create a more equal society—could eventually grow.

Overview of the Field

The most articulate historian of the republican tradition was Jules Michelet,* whose *The History of the French Revolution* emphasized the importance of the unknown, ordinary people of history.[4] Lefebvre shared Michelet's belief that the revolution was created as much by the mass of ordinary individuals as by political leaders. Like Michelet, Lefebvre understood the revolution partly as a moral—even a spiritual—event, comparing its growth to the establishment of early Christianity.[5]

Counterrevolutionary interpretations were revived at the end of the nineteenth century by the philosopher and critic Hippolyte Taine.* Taine wrote a damning account of the revolution, arguing that it was based on empty ideas and driven by manipulative elite classes.[6] In the years between World War I* and World War II* these views were restated in France by the historians Jacques Bainville* and Pierre Gaxotte,* both members of a monarchist (that is, pro-monarchy) organization known as *Action Française*.*[7] This group was anti-republican, hostile toward Jews, counterrevolutionary, and deeply nationalistic (that is, it held an extremely patriotic belief in the inherent superiority of France). Following the defeat of France by the Germans in 1940, their views were seen as important by the new Vichy* government, which aimed to replace the chaos of 1789 with a new *révolution nationale*, or national revolution.[8]

The Marxist interpretation proposed that the revolution had seen a transition between two distinct periods of world history: from feudalism* (the system where landowners protected laborers who worked in their fields for little or no personal reward) to capitalism. In the main, the class driving this change and also benefitting from it were the bourgeoisie—the propertied, wealthy, middle class. This idea was adapted by a later generation of Marxists that included Jean Jaurès, a leading nineteenth-century politician and author of the first socialist history of the revolution. Unlike those Marxists who believed the unjust capitalist system could only be broken if there was a new revolution led by the industrial working classes (the proletariat),* Jaurès believed that a socialist society could be created within the framework of the existing democratic republic.[9]

Academic Influences

In 1937 Lefebvre was named the Chair of the History of the French Revolution at the Sorbonne.* This prestigious post had been created in 1885 for the radical republican historian Alphonse Aulard.* The professors who followed Aulard into the position were expected to write history that kept alive the spirit of the Third Republic*—the constitutional settlement dating from 1870, founded on ideas of equality before the law and freedom of expression, and owing something to the spirit of the revolution. Lefebvre was no exception: his account of the revolution married republican thought, with its emphasis on national unity, to theoretical ideas borrowed from Marx.

Lefebvre's predecessor in mixing the republican and the Marxist approaches had been Jaurès. Both men borrowed Marx's notion of class struggle—that historical change is driven by conflict between different social groups, fighting for control over the resources and tools required for production—but they did not simply reduce history to a conflict between competing material interests. The past also had a moral dimension, and both men emphasized the free will of the individual and the fact that moral choices could be made.

Jaurès was also a pioneer of social and economic history, looking to document how the revolution impacted the quality of living of the lower orders. He was a founder of the *Commission d'histoire économique de la Révolution française* (Commission of Economic History on the French Revolution) in 1905. Over the coming decades, the commission published materials relating to economic history, as well as electoral lists and *cahiers de doléances** (registers of grievances). Lefebvre began corresponding with the commission from 1904 onwards and drew on many of these sources to write *The Coming of the French Revolution* in 1939. Lefebvre said that if he had a master, then it was Jaurès.[10]

NOTES

1   Abbé Augustin Barruel, *Mémoires pour server à l'histoire du Jacobinisme* (Paris, 1797–8).

2   Pierre Gaxotte, *La Révolution française* (Paris: Fayard,1928); Léon Daudet, *Deux idoles sanguinaires: La Révolution et son fils Bonaparte* (Paris: Albin Michel, 1939); Jacques Bainville, *Histoire de France* (Paris: Fayard, 1924).

3   Karl Marx, *Contribution to the Critique of Hegel's Philosophy of Right* (1843) and *On the Jewish Question* (1843–4).

4   Jules Michelet, *Histoire de la Révolution française*, 7 vols. (Paris, 1847–53).

5   Georges Lefebvre, *The Coming of the French Revolution*, trans. Robert R. Palmer (Princeton, NJ: Princeton University Press, 2005), 213.

6   Hippolyte Taine, *Les Origines de la France contemporaine*, 5 vols. (Paris, 1875–93).

7   Gaxotte, La Révolution française; Bainville, *Histoire de France*.

8   See Stephen Wilson, "A View of the Past: Action Française Historiography and its Socio-political Function," *Historical Journal* 19 (1976): 135–61.

9   Jean Jaurès, *Histoire socialiste de la Révolution française*, ed. A. Mathiez, 8 vols. (Paris: Libre de l'Humanité, 1922–4).

10 Stéphane Buzzi, "Georges Lefebvre (1874–1959), ou une histoire sociale possible", *Le Mouvement Social*, no. 200 (2002–3): 186.

MODULE 3
THE PROBLEM

KEY POINTS

- In *The Coming of the French Revolution*, Lefebvre tried to show why the old regime*—roughly, monarchy* and aristocracy*—fell apart in 1789, and who benefited from its demise.

- He joined a fierce debate in which conservatives stressed the accidental and unnecessarily bloody nature of 1789. Radicals saw the revolution as a bourgeois* or middle-class uprising that failed to deliver real social reform.

- Lefebvre saw the French Revolution* as necessary and saw it as the result of social tension throughout the whole nation.

Core Question

The question at the heart of Georges Lefebvre's *The Coming of the French Revolution* had been troubling scholars for generations: why did the authority of the French monarchy—the Bourbon dynasty*—collapse so dramatically in 1789?

France had been ruled by the Bourbons since Henri IV came to the throne in 1589; prior to the revolution, they had been the most powerful royal dynasty on the European continent. The French monarchy stood at the summit of an entire social structure made up of corporate bodies*—the legal system, the guilds, the academies, and the *parlements** (or bodies of magistrates)—that had existed for centuries. The whole infrastructure of the French state relied on the king. In 1789, it was not only the authority of the monarchy that was called into question, but the whole infrastructure he ruled over too.

❝ The Old Regime did not bend before the juridical revolution. Having taken to force, it was destroyed by force, which the people, descending into the street, put at the service of what they regarded as right, though even their own representatives had not dared to ask such assistance from them. ❞

Georges Lefebvre, *The Coming of the French Revolution*

By 1786, the monarchy was bankrupt. Reform would be necessary to restore the kingdom's finances. Answering the question of the monarchy's collapse is a matter of understanding why these attempts at reform spiraled out of the king's control and exploded into revolution in 1789. The months of frantic political activity between 1787 and 1789 were crucial and would later be dubbed the French "pre-revolution" by the historian Jean Egret.*[1] For Georges Lefebvre, it was not just a question of understanding the mistakes made by the king and his ministers at this time. The French Revolution, he says in the work, was also a social revolution caused by widespread conflicts within French society as a whole.

Some scholars had looked at the monarchy's long-term political problems, but this was not Lefebvre's objective. Instead he took an in-depth look at the events of the one key year of 1789, describing how a series of crises that year saw the old regime's authority disintegrate.

The Participants

While Lefebvre was very aware of the nineteenth-century accounts of the revolution by leading republican* historians such as Jules Michelet,* he wanted to deploy a more scientific kind of history himself. If Michelet was famed for his dazzling use of words and poetic descriptions, Lefebvre was determined to stay true to the archival record. Like the historian Alphonse Aulard* before him, he believed in the need to study original documents closely. Lefebvre, however, wanted to expand the definition of what kind of original documents should be looked at in the first place. Thanks to Jean Jaurès,* socialist* history had broken fresh ground in analyzing the materials related to economic conditions and everyday life, showing how even the humblest citizens experienced the revolution. Along these lines, Albert Mathiez* produced extensive studies on a crisis in the cost of living in Paris between 1792 and 1794.[2]

Lefebvre had been appointed to a position at the University of Strasbourg in 1928 and had discovered the methods of the *Annales** historians; they not only wanted to use more documentary evidence from the time in their historical work, but also wanted to bring history into closer relationship with the social sciences* such as sociology and economics. Lefebvre was heavily influenced by the work of the economic historian Ernest Labrousse.* Labrousse used statistical analysis to demonstrate that economic hardship caused by bad harvests and the rising price of food led to an industrial recession before the French Revolution. By tracking how the price of grain fluctuated, Labrousse could demonstrate that bread reached its highest price in 1789, causing severe hardship for many. His findings were published in 1937 and Lefebvre used Labrousse's conclusions to prove the connection between the economic and the political crises of 1789.[3]

The Contemporary Debate

Against its critics, Lefebvre wanted to resist the idea that the revolution was marked by failure. Many liberal commentators who were committed to protecting individual freedoms tended to praise the early years of the revolution, but then criticized the turn towards the dictatorship of the Jacobins*—a political group that emerged during the revolution and which would do anything to save the republic after

1792. The American historian Crane Brinton* had published a particularly important book called *Anatomy of Revolution* in 1938, in which he claimed there existed a fixed pattern in revolutions that moderates would inevitably be displaced by extremists before things ultimately came full circle and everything returned to order.[4] Lefebvre, however, does not agree that the peaceful beginnings of the revolution were sabotaged or derailed by the Terror*—the period between 1792 and 1794 in which thousands were accused of "counterrevolutionary" tendencies and executed. The violence of the Terror, he argues, was already an important part of the revolt of 1789.

In part, this was because the revolution had been driven forward by the power of the masses and the fear that this created among the elites. Lefebvre highlighted three decisive events of 1789 where the power of the crowds helped topple the old regime. First was the attack on the Bastille* fortress—which acted as both a prison and an arsenal—in July 1789, in which many Parisian artisans took part. Second, there were the disturbances all over the French countryside in June, July, and August where the peasants refused to pay their taxes and set fire to property belonging to the elite. Third, there were the "October Days,"* in which crowds marched to the royal palace of Versailles* on October 5 and 6 to demand bread. This group included market women who marched alongside the National Guard,* a military force that had emerged earlier in the year to uphold law and order. They forced the royal family to return to the capital under escort.

Taken together, these three events forced many frightened aristocrats (those who held rank and privilege, often inherited) to go further with reforms than they had initially wanted to.[5]

NOTES

1   Jean Egret, *La Prérévolution française* (Paris: Presses Universitaires de France, 1962).

2   Albert Mathiez, *La Vie chère et le mouvement social sous la Terreur* (Paris: Fayard, 1927).

3   Georges Lefebvre, "Les Mouvements des prix et les origines de la Révolution française," *Annales historiques de la Révolution française* 9 (1937): 288–239.

4   Crane Brinton, *The Anatomy of Revolution* (New York: Norton, 1938).

5   Georges Lefebvre, *The Coming of the French Revolution*, trans. Robert R. Palmer (Princeton, NJ: Princeton University Press, 2005), 209.

MODULE 4
THE AUTHOR'S CONTRIBUTION

KEY POINTS

- Lefebvre believes that the French Revolution* emerged from conflict between four social groups—the aristocracy* (the privileged ruling class), the bourgeoisie* (the wealthy, propertied, middle class), the urban masses, and the peasants.

- He highlights the behavior of ordinary people in both towns and countryside. Their sometimes-violent actions ensured that the ideas and principles on which the revolution started were eventually carried into law.

- Lefebvre builds on the work of previous historians, who stressed economic factors as an important reason for the revolution. But Lefebvre himself paints the revolution as a complex, multi-layered event.

Author's Aims

Georges Lefebvre's *The Coming of the French Revolution* is an attempt to provide a short and clear account of why the absolutist* monarchy*—in which the king was the source of all authority— collapsed in 1789. Combining a mix of narrative and analysis, Lefebvre reconstructs the events of a single, turbulent year. The book is influenced by a number of different historical approaches. From the theory of Marxism,* in which current economic and social systems would be replaced by fairer ones, Lefebvre borrows the idea of class struggle,* the conflict between different social groups. He understands the crisis of 1789 as rising from long-standing tensions, especially between the nobility with their inherited privileges and the bourgeoisie, who were people who had made their own wealth.

> 66 The first act of the Revolution, in 1788, consisted in a triumph of the aristocracy, which, taking advantage of the government crisis, hoped to reassert itself ... But, after having paralyzed the royal power which upheld its own social preeminence, the aristocracy opened the way to the bourgeois revolution, then to the popular revolution in the cities and finally to the revolution of the peasants—and found itself buried under the ruins of the Old Regime. 99
>
> Georges Lefebvre, *The Coming of the French Revolution*

From the influential *Annales** historians, Lefebvre takes the view that history as a discipline should be closely linked to the social sciences.* He shares the Jacobin* and republican* historians' belief that the revolution represented a moment of liberation, not just for France, but perhaps for all mankind.

The revolution was not about one particular group or the achievement of a minority. It was a short-lived moment of "national unity embracing all parts of the French territory and all classes of Frenchmen, a unity for which the monarchy had long labored and which it was the glory of the National Assembly* to achieve."[1]

This bringing together of different approaches reflected Lefebvre's desire to write an interpretation of the revolution which could satisfy scholars, but also appeal to a wide public. He had acted as an advisor to the government for the celebrations marking the 150th anniversary of the French Revolution that took place in 1939 and had also been a consultant on the French filmmaker Jean Renoir's* *La Marseillaise* in 1938, a work that celebrated the heroism of ordinary French citizens in 1789.[2] In *The Coming of the French Revolution*, Lefebvre insisted on the central importance of the "popular revolution," the spontaneous and patriotic uprisings in towns and villages across France. The revolution was therefore something that belonged to all modern French men and women, something that their ancestors had fought for and in which they should take pride.

Approach

The four-part structure of Lefebvre's book mirrored one of his central arguments: that the revolution was caused by the independent actions of four separate social groups: the aristocracy, the bourgeoisie, the urban workers, and the peasants. To understand why the revolution happened, it was vital to understand the motivations and behavior of each group. It was also vital to understand how their actions affected one another. Lefebvre's layered approach revealed the many different factors that came together to produce the revolution. By studying the issues that motivated each class, Lefebvre deftly introduced the economic, ideological, and political concerns that interested and divided eighteenth-century French society.

Lefebvre approaches the revolution through the lens of social history,* believing that the actions of ordinary men and women in 1789 were as important as the actions of political elites. His research into the peasant revolution was particularly innovative; although not the first historian to argue that the peasants' actions mattered, he backed up his observations with an unprecedented level of research. Moreover, while the communist* historian Albert Mathiez* had studied the economic and social conditions in cities during the French Revolution,[3] Lefebvre extends that to the countryside. This was a deviation from Marxist orthodoxy; while Marx* believed that revolutions grew out of urban, industrial action, Lefebvre stressed that what happened in the countryside in 1789 was as important to the revolution as what happened in the cities.

Contribution in Context

Lefebvre built on the work of previous historians. His argument that 1789 came about because of a clash between different social classes had been commonplace from the time of the revolution onwards. Historians of the early nineteenth century, among them François-Auguste Mignet* and François Guizot,* believed that class struggle had been occurring in France since the Middle Ages. For these historians, however, class identity was rooted in ethnic identity. They saw the tension as a struggle between Germanic peoples—the conquering Franks—and the defeated natives, the Gauls.[4]

Later historians followed Karl Marx in reinterpreting class in both social and economic terms. The socialist* leader and historian Jean Jaurès* was also convinced that the French Revolution marked the arrival of the capitalist* bourgeoisie into power. He interpreted the revolution as marking the threshold between two different economic systems: the feudalism* of the Old Regime* and the capitalism of the post-revolutionary order.[5] The transition between these two systems was inevitably messy.

In *The Coming of the French Revolution*, Lefebvre claimed that from the fourteenth century onwards, a bourgeois class had been growing, enjoying prosperity in trade and flourishing in law and in administration. This produced a situation that was bound to cause conflict, where the rising bourgeoisie had wealth, but the aristocracy maintained a tight grip on political and symbolic power. "The Revolution of 1789 restored the harmony between fact and law," said Lefebvre.[6] On finally gaining power, the bourgeoisie were determined to destroy all the institutions that had blocked their rise. For Lefebvre these class tensions explained why the revolutionaries sought not just to limit the power of the king, but to sweep away the entire social structure of the Old Regime.

NOTES

1 Georges Lefebvre, *The Coming of the French Revolution*, trans. Robert R. Palmer (Princeton, NJ: Princeton University Press, 2005), 166.

2 Pascal Ory, *Une Nation pour la mémoire: 1889, 1939, 1989, trois jubilés révolutionnaires* (Paris: Presses de la Fondation nationale des sciences politiques, 1992), 71–2.

3 Albert Mathiez, *La Vie chère et le mouvement social sous la Terreur* (Paris: Fayard, 1927).

4 See Ceri Crossley, *French Historians and Romanticism: Thierry, Guizot, the Saint-Simonians, Quinet, Michelet* (New York and London: Routledge, 2002).

5 Jean Jaurès, *Histoire socialiste de la Révolution française*, ed. Albert Mathiez, 8 vols. (Paris: Libre de l'Humanité, 1922–4).

6 Lefebvre, *The Coming of the French Revolution*, 2.

SECTION 2
IDEAS

MODULE 5
MAIN IDEAS

KEY POINTS

- Lefebvre's main aim was to explain why the political crisis related to the monarchy* was resolved with major social transformation rather than simple checks on royal power.

- He thought the French Revolution* happened because of four distinct but interconnected conflicts between rival social groups.

- This four-fold approach influenced the structure of the book. Lefebvre looked first at how dissent spread in each group, then at how unrest became irresistible as all these causes merged.

Key Themes

In *The Coming of The French Revolution*, Georges Lefebvre argues that the French Revolution developed as a four-fold process; he identifies four social classes—the aristocracy,* the bourgeoisie,* the urban crowds, and the rural peasantry—and argues that these four groups played leading roles in four separate challenges to traditional rule.

The political crisis began in 1787 as a clash between the aristocracy and the monarchy over tax reform. It spread in 1789 to the convening of the Estates General*—an assembly made up of representatives of the clergy, the nobility, and commoners, which had not convened since 1614. This led to a constitutional revolt by the deputies* representing the bourgeoisie. In order to secure the reforms they were promised at this assembly, the urban classes in towns and cities across France improvised new forms of authority and attacked royal fortifications. Finally, in the summer of 1789, peasants refused to pay

❝ The Revolution of 1789 consisted first of all in the fall of the absolute monarchy and the advent of a liberty henceforth guaranteed by constitutional government ... But it was also the advent of equality before the law, without which liberty would be but another privilege of the powerful. For the French of 1789 liberty and equality were inseparable, almost two words for the same thing ... ❞

Georges Lefebvre, *The Coming of the French Revolution*

their taxes and rose up against local manor houses in protest at the feudal* system. These groups were acting on their own, each pursuing their own goals and ambitions, to create four different challenges for the monarchy.

Although the revolution came about because of these four interconnected crises, Lefebvre argues that 1789 was essentially a bourgeois revolution: it was bourgeois values that were mainly expressed by the new National Assembly* and then passed into law (what Lefebvre called the "juridical revolution").[1] Many of the new laws passed by the National Assembly upheld bourgeois ideals: rewards based on merit, fairer taxation, equality before the law, freedom of thought, property rights, free trade. Lefebvre insists, however, that the bourgeoisie could not have brought down the monarchy alone—and they would not have wanted to. A real revolution needed everyone who had a political interest to be involved: "Only a mass movement could seal the ruin of the Old Regime"* (the monarchy and the institutional influence of the aristocratic class).[2]

Exploring the Ideas

In his narrative, Lefebvre gives each of the four social groups—aristocracy, bourgeoisie, urban crowds, rural peasantry—their own character. Each group had interests that conflicted with those of other classes. Lefebvre believed that throughout the eighteenth century the nobility had seen their privileged position in royal institutions eroded as talented commoners pushed them out of important posts.[3] By refusing to cooperate with the king over taxation in 1787–8, in Lefebvre's view the nobility was aiming to humiliate the crown and to recapture some of its former power. However, few nobles were prepared for the radical anti-aristocratic laws to bring about legal and fiscal equality that were introduced by the National Assembly from 1789.[4]

Lefebvre's analysis of the bourgeoisie was controversial. In describing this class, he drew on some elements proposed by Karl Marx,* interpreting them as a force of dynamic capitalists* who wanted to modernize the French economy. He also borrowed from the German sociologist Max Weber* to view them as champions of rational, scientific thought and values that were not based in religion. Above all, Lefebvre associates the bourgeoisie with the views of the Enlightenment,* the late seventeenth- and early eighteenth-century movement that saw reason as the best means to improve society. The Enlightenment was a "great stream of ideas" that for Lefebvre embodies "the ascendancy of the bourgeoisie" and the "common ideal that summarized the evolution of western civilization."[5] The ideals of the Declaration of the Rights of Man,* a document enshrining human rights that was adopted as law by the government in 1789, showed a "triumphant class full of energy and on the way to transforming the world," convinced that it "was destined forever to assure the welfare and progress of the human race."[6] In the short term it was bourgeois values and, therefore, the bourgeois class that triumphed in 1789.

The defiance of the aristocracy and the bourgeoisie against the king though would have been crushed by the royal troops had it not been for the outbreak of the popular revolution. It was the twin rebellion of the Parisian crowds in July and the peasants in the countryside that definitively killed off the Old Regime.

The masses were not fighting to uphold bourgeois values. They were haunted by paranoid fears of an "aristocratic plot" to keep them down. Lefebvre highlighted how far the Parisian crowds embraced forms of government that were completely opposed to bourgeois principles: direct democracy,* popular justice, and a citizen militia.[7] The peasants did not share bourgeois ideas of property either, being highly protective of common land and economic regulation, and did not pay much attention to what the National Assembly had to say.[8] The peasants did not owe their gains to what the bourgeois elite said, writes Lefebvre: "They liberated themselves, and the successive Assemblies only sanctioned what they accomplished."[9]

Language and Expression

The structure of *The Coming of the Revolution* perfectly captures the sense of an unfolding drama, in which each group plays their part.

The four crises followed one after the other, each deepening the problems of the monarchy. There was no guiding intelligence or single leader driving the process forward. Many of the revolution's iconic earlier leaders, such as Honoré-Gabriel Riqueti de Mirabeau,* an excellent speaker, and the Abbé Sieyès,* a cleric and political writer, either failed to support or actively condemned key decisions and were quickly sidelined by fast-moving events.[10] Lefebvre's account helps us feel the messiness of revolutionary situations, where power is highly unstable and each group has to keep adjusting to unexpected developments.

The text is written clearly and concisely for the general reader, and these virtues have been preserved in Robert Palmer's translation from 1947. Most usefully, Lefebvre cleverly identifies what was "at stake" in 1789. The revolutionaries were not simply fighting for concessions in law. After all, on June 23, 1789 King Louis XVI* had been willing to reform taxation, make finances accountable, grant liberty of the press, and create provincial assemblies. He was unwilling to tinker with traditional social structures.[11] For Lefebvre, the revolution was truly important because it refused to accept that the aristocracy, or any other group, could remain a law unto itself, a "nation within the nation." It was because such privileges had to be swept away that the "character" of the revolution was "not so much political as social."[12]

NOTES

1 Georges Lefebvre, *The Coming of the French Revolution*, trans. Robert R. Palmer (Princeton, NJ: Princeton University Press, 2005), 67.

2 Lefebvre, *The Coming of the French Revolution*, 189.

3 Lefebvre, *The Coming of the French Revolution*, 15–19.

4 Lefebvre, *The Coming of the French Revolution*, 207.

5 Lefebvre, *The Coming of the French Revolution*, 213.

6 Lefebvre, *The Coming of the French Revolution*, 175–6.

7 Lefebvre, *The Coming of the French Revolution*, 118–20, 190, 192–3.

8 Lefebvre, *The Coming of the French Revolution*, 157.

9 Lefebvre, *The Coming of the French Revolution*, 208, 211.

10 Lefebvre, *The Coming of the French Revolution*, 164, 187.

11 Lefebvre, *The Coming of the French Revolution*, 84–5.

12 Lefebvre, *The Coming of the French Revolution*, 209.

MODULE 6
SECONDARY IDEAS

KEY POINTS

- Lefebvre believed that while social issues drove the French Revolution,* the characters of individuals at the heart of the action also played a part in how things unfolded.

- Lefebvre was certain that the events of 1789 clearly indicated that there would be violence later as the principles of the revolution came under threat.

- *The Coming of the French Revolution* claims that people were motivated not only by how the revolution could benefit them personally, but also by political principles.

Other Ideas

While he believed the French Revolution was rooted in social and economic frictions, Georges Lefebvre clearly states in *The Coming of the French Revolution* that individuals played a key role in shaping the course of events.

King Louis XVI,* for example, was honest and well-intentioned, but lacked the intellectual qualities required of him. Long before 1789, he and his hated wife Marie-Antoinette* were already "the laughing-stock of his courtiers."[1] Lefebvre argued that if Louis XVI had been a different person, the events of 1789 would probably have taken quite a different turn. The king's lack of leadership and arrogant manner sapped his authority with the Estates General* (a national representative assembly convened for the first time since 1614). In the October Days* of 1789, his unwillingness to flee, as crowds from Paris marched to the palace at Versailles* demanding bread, ended with him being forcibly held by the crowds and

❝ The elements in the revolutionary complex cannot be taken apart. Revolution is a bloc, a single thing. The moralist must praise heroism and condemn cruelty; but the moralist does not explain events. **❞**

Georges Lefebvre, *The Coming of the French Revolution*

dragged back to Paris.[2] Lefebvre's arguments show that he believed chance and individual character played their part in bringing about the revolution.

The Coming of the French Revolution is packed with minor observations and asides that would become central to later historiography. Lefebvre frequently situates the crisis in France in relation to other nations, whether it is the defeat of the group of Dutch patriots looking to change the political system in their country in 1787, the influence of the American Revolution* against British rule, or the example of the Glorious Revolution* of 1688 in Britain,[3] in which King James II was overthrown by William III and parliamentary authority was reinforced. While the book focuses on the events of one year, there are numerous anticipations of and allusions to what would come next. Lefebvre suggests the year 1789 contained the seeds of what was to come. He argues, for instance, that the property rights gained in 1789 were so important to the bourgeoisie that in 1799 they were willing to embrace a military dictator—Napoleon Bonaparte*—in order to protect them.[4]

Exploring the Ideas

The most striking of Lefebvre's allusions to later events concerns the place of political violence. He insists throughout the work that the hand of the elite classes was forced. The vote for the abolition of feudalism* that was decreed on August 4, 1789, for example, where the nobility consented to give up their privileges, was due to hard-

43

nosed calculations and the fear of turmoil in the countryside.[5] To that extent, Lefebvre believed that the Terror* which dominated France between 1792 and 1794, in the course of which many thousands were executed on the grounds of their political beliefs and affiliations, was not a freak accident that betrayed the principles of 1789. According to Lefebvre, the opening months of the revolution were full of omens of the bloodshed that was to come, especially in a context where violence was politically necessary and where fears of an "aristocratic* plot" were sweeping the country.

This meant that Lefebvre referred to the royal minister Calonne*— who was chased out of the country by a civic body known as a *parlement** after his reform programs of 1786–7 had been rejected—as the first émigré.*[6] There was already talk on July 13, the day before the revolution began in earnest with the storming of the Bastille* (an arsenal and prison on the edge of Paris that had come to represent royal tyranny), of "exterminating all nobles".[7] The artisans of Paris tried to introduce a kind of "direct democracy"* and steps were taken to found a "popular revolutionary tribunal"* that would speed up the sentencing of enemies of the revolution. Elected representatives were also involved in the first acts of violence, defending the people and their behavior while marching with the heads of their enemies on pikes. They argued that all legal niceties had to be suspended when the nation was in a state of war.[8] By 1792, people's fears in 1789 of plots to undermine the revolution had become a reality. Lefebvre understood the Terror as a defensive measure to protect the revolution from enemies both within and without.[9]

Overlooked

The sheer number of ideas in Lefebvre's work means that some have been overlooked; often, he alludes to an idea—the new meeting places that sprang up in the eighteenth century, for example—that he does not then continue to study in detail.

Lefebvre believed that the revolutionary call for equality grew out of the Enlightenment* (the contemporary intellectual movement emphasizing that reason should be used to improve human society). Lefebvre said that eighteenth-century cafes, scientific circles, and societies formed to do good—such as the Freemasons,* a quasi-secret society open to professionals—helped to spread these Enlightenment ideas.[10] Thirty years later the influential German sociologist Jürgen Habermas* outlined how these new city spaces allowed for the emergence of a "public sphere," where for the first time people could openly debate and criticize the actions of the monarchy*[11]—but the idea is also there in Lefebvre.

Lefebvre has been caricatured as a rigid Marxist* by some historians, who have overlooked the subtleties of his work as a consequence. His use of materialist* explanations—that is, roughly, his position that events could be explained by an analysis of struggles between different sections of French society over wealth and resources—for the rebellion of 1789 did not mean that he thought people were solely motivated by what they could get out of the revolution. "Reality is mutilated if we overlook the play of practical interests in producing the revolutionary spirit," he writes. However, Lefebvre cautions that "we should commit no less an error in forgetting that there is no true revolutionary spirit without the idealism that alone inspires sacrifice."[12]

His time with the *Annales*★ historians in Strasbourg in 1928 had deepened his interest in the power of collective psychology[13]—the motivations and desires of the masses. Lefebvre often compared the revolution to the beginnings of Christianity in the devotion it inspired among its followers. According to him, the revolution did not preserve and improve on the Christian message of brotherhood; it was also an "invitation to a life of sainthood."[14] These arguments show what Lefebvre had in mind when he argued that political principles could not be reduced to simple economic interests; for him, all true revolutionary action took place "in the realm of the spirit."[15]

NOTES

1   Georges Lefebvre, *The Coming of the French Revolution*, trans. Robert R. Palmer (Princeton, NJ: Princeton University Press, 2005), 25.

2   Lefebvre, *The Coming of the French Revolution*, 72, 84, 200.

3   Lefebvre, *The Coming of the French Revolution*, 32, 36, 212.

4   Lefebvre, *The Coming of the French Revolution*, 212.

5   Lefebvre, *The Coming of the French Revolution*, 156–9.

6   Lefebvre, *The Coming of the French Revolution*, 34.

7   Lefebvre, *The Coming of the French Revolution*, 116.

8   Lefebvre, *The Coming of the French Revolution*, 116–20.

9   Lefebvre, *The Coming of the French Revolution*, 211.

10 Lefebvre, *The Coming of the French Revolution*, 47.

11 Jürgen Habermas, *The Structural Transformation of the Public Sphere: An Inquiry into a Category of Bourgeois Society*, trans. Thomas Burger (Cambridge: Polity Press,1989).

12 Lefebvre, *The Coming of the French Revolution*, 48.

13 See Patrick Hutton, *History as an Art of Memory* (Hanover: University of Vermont, 1993), 135–43.

14 Lefebvre, *The Coming of the French Revolution*, 218.

15 Lefebvre, *The Coming of the French Revolution*, 209.

MODULE 7
ACHIEVEMENT

KEY POINTS

- *The Coming of the French Revolution* provided an overall interpretation of the origins of the French Revolution,* crafting the experience of distinct groups into an impressive single narrative.

- Lefebvre was a major influence on scholars in other countries as they considered the political roles played by men and women of the "lower" classes.

- His subtle argument and commitment to data was sometimes at odds with his separating of French society into four distinct groups. The evidence suggests that the reality was less clear-cut than that.

Assessing the Argument

Writing *The Coming of the French Revolution,* Georges Lefebvre wanted to present a coherent account of the origins of the French Revolution. In the book he showed that the revolution could not be understood simply by looking at the political elites; it came about because of uncoordinated acts of defiance from four separate social groups and succeeded because it was a collective, popular uprising.

Lefebvre wove the experiences of these distinct groups into a single narrative, highlighting the changing social, political, and economic conditions of eighteenth-century France. The American historian Robert R. Palmer* and Lefebvre's fellow Frenchman Jacques Godechot* both borrowed from Lefebvre's analysis of the French situation to try to make comparisons with the situations of other nations. Perhaps, they suggested, 1789 was one defining moment in an "age of democratic revolution" or in an interconnected "Atlantic

> ❝ The bourgeoisie put its emphasis on earthly happiness and on the dignity of man; it urged the necessity of increasing the former and elevating the latter, through the control of natural forces by science and the utilizing of them to augment the general wealth. ... The conception was dynamic, calling upon all men, without distinction of birth, to enter into a universal competition from which the progress of mankind was to follow without end. ❞
>
> Georges Lefebvre, *The Coming of the French Revolution*

Revolution," with numerous groups demanding change in Europe, Africa, North America and South America.[1]

Lefebvre's social interpretation of 1789 was widely accepted until the 1960s; then some of his arguments were attacked in the 1960s, the 1970s, and the 1980s. As social history came back into fashion in the 1990s, historians again started to pay close attention to Lefebvre's point of view, as did scholars from other disciplines. The American political scientist James Scott's* famous discussion of peasant resistance in South Asia, *Weapons of the Weak* (1985),[2] used anecdotes from Lefebvre's research into the peasant uprising to help demonstrate the ways in which violence can be used to enforce community norms.

Lefebvre's ideas about *why* the revolution happened have influenced the work of social scientists like Theda Skocpol* and Charles Tilly,* who have used these ideas to understand what kind of structure of society could lead to revolution.[3] Like his peers in the French *Annales** school, Lefebvre was in favor of closer relations between historians and social scientists* such as psychologists, sociologists, and social anthropologists.[4] He would have welcomed this dialogue with other disciplines.

Achievement in Context

Lefebvre, well known for his scholarship, was keen to provide a defense of the *values* of the revolution. This aspect of the book helped him to appeal, in particular, to fellow socialists,* who shared his interest in the poor and the exploited. His methods and influence in writing "history from below"*—events as seen through the eyes of everyday people— can be seen in many other left-wing* accounts of how the lower classes in society developed a political awareness. The work of the influential British historians Eric Hobsbawm,* on banditry, and E. P. Thompson, on labor history, are both good examples.[5] Another historian who learned much from Lefebvre was George Rudé,* who studied the politics of crowd behavior and dedicated his works to Lefebvre.[6]

The Coming of the French Revolution was little known in France for many years. Its left-wing take on the revolution of 1789 was considered subversive by the right-wing Vichy* government (the government in occupied France during World War II,* based in the French city of Vichy). The book was suppressed; eight thousand copies were burned and it was not to be reissued in French until 1970. The book enjoyed very wide international circulation in the English-speaking world, however, thanks to a translation by Robert R. Palmer,* published in 1947. It was the most effective and most readable introduction to the French Revolution and was used on many American university campuses.

Lefebvre was a warm and supportive colleague to many young British and American scholars who wanted to study the revolution. Richard Cobb,* a British social historian of the revolution, described visiting Lefebvre in his home in the Parisian suburb of Boulogne-Billancourt shortly after World War II. Surrounded by images of socialist leader Jean Jaurès* and the 1789 revolutionary Maximilien Robespierre,* Lefebvre seemed the "living embodiment of republican* rectitude, of lay probity, a sort of French Abraham Lincoln* dressed in antiquated clothes."[7]

Limitations

Despite his wide reading, Lefebvre presents a slightly outdated account of the development of the eighteenth-century economy. Following on from Marx* and Jaurès, he argues that the French Revolution marked the transition between "feudal"* and "capitalist"* systems of production. Yet according to Lefebvre's own description, France in 1789 was "a society in which modern capitalism was barely beginning" and where waged workers had "no clear consciousness of class."[8] Those investing in projects in mining, foundries, iron smelting, or glass making, or speculating on the stock market, were in the minority; these pursuits were as often led by the aristocracy* as by the merchants of the bourgeoisie.*[9] Once again, it was difficult to tell the classes apart, because the nobility and the bourgeoisie seemed to share ties of marriage, commercial interest, and social contact. If this was the case, how could Lefebvre argue that the revolution had been caused by the bourgeoisie's "common detestation of the aristocracy"?[10]

Was the expansion of capitalism a cause or a consequence of the French Revolution? In the 1950s and 1960s these problems of definition surrounding class and capitalism would be seized on by historians who questioned old beliefs. Revisionists* like Alfred Cobban* (that is, historians questioning the orthodox interpretations of historical events) questioned whether there really had been a rising bourgeoisie trying to seize power in 1789.[11] In the 1970s historians such as François Furet* criticized the search for any social explanations of the revolution as misguided, and encouraged their colleagues to turn their attentions instead to the role of political languages and ideologies.[12]

In these often bitter exchanges, Lefebvre was unfairly characterized as a rigid and inflexible Marxist.* *The Coming of the French Revolution* was admired as a survey of events, but its ideas about social struggle were sometimes viewed as misguided.

NOTES

1   Robert R. Palmer, *The Age of Democratic Revolutions: A Political History of Europe and America 1760–1800*, 2 vols. (Princeton, NJ: Princeton University Press, 1964); Jacques Godechot, *France and the Atlantic Revolution of the Eighteenth Century* (New York: The Free Press, 1965).

2   John C. Scott, *Weapons of the Weak: Everyday Forms of Peasant Resistance* (New Haven, CT, and London: Yale University Press, 1985), 270.

3   Theda Skocpol, *States and Social Revolutions: A Comparative Analysis of France, Russia and China* (Cambridge: Cambridge University Press, 1979); and Charles Tilly, *The Vendée* (Cambridge, MA: Harvard University Press, 1964).

4   Georges Lefebvre, "Avenir de l'histoire," in Études sur la Révolution française (Paris: Presses Universitaires de France, 1954), 6.

5   Eric Hobsbawm, *Primitive Rebels: Studies in Archaic Forms of Social Movement in the Nineteenth and Twentieth Centuries* (Manchester: Manchester University Press, 1959); E. P. Thompson, *The Making of the English Working Class* (London: Victor Gollancz, 1963).

6   George Rudé, *The Crowd in the French Revolution* (Oxford: Oxford University Press, 1959).

7   Richard Cobb, "Georges Lefebvre," in *A Second Identity: Essays on France and French History* (Oxford: Oxford University Press, 1969), 84–100.

8   Georges Lefebvre, *The Coming of the French Revolution*, trans. Robert R. Palmer (Princeton, NJ: Princeton University Press, 2005), 97, 216.

9   Lefebvre, *The Coming of the French Revolution*, 13–14.

10 Lefebvre, *The Coming of the French Revolution*, 43–6.

11 Alfred Cobban, *Aspects of the French Revolution* (London: Jonathan Cape, 1968).

12 François Furet, *Interpreting the French Revolution* (Cambridge: Cambridge University Press, 1981).

MODULE 8
PLACE IN THE AUTHOR'S WORK

KEY POINTS

- Lefebvre's pioneering work on the peasantry is more innovative than the broader overviews of the French Revolution* that he produced towards the end of his life.

- *The Coming of the French Revolution* was a distillation of Lefebvre's early research, which showed understanding of how social issues and rural tensions could help people understand the revolution as a whole.

- *The Coming of the French Revolution* was highly respected in Britain and North America, thanks to a translation by Robert R. Palmer, from 1947. It became well known in France again when it was republished in 1970.

Positioning

The central concern of Georges Lefebvre's *The Coming of the French Revolution*—the revolutionary events of 1789—was an abiding concern for the whole of his academic life. In 1932 Lefebvre published *La Grande Peur de 1789* (The Great Fear of 1789), a book examining the paranoid rumors that spread amongst the peasantry before the outbreak of the revolution.[1] The peasants believed that there was an aristocratic* plot against them. This fear was largely baseless, but Lefebvre recognized that it still helped to explain why the peasants chose to revolt. Through this he came to argue that it was as important to study mindsets as it was to study hard facts. *The Great Fear* was highly influenced by Lefebvre's time spent at Strasbourg among the *Annales** historians; this influence was also evident in Lefebvre's essay "Les Foules révolutionnaires" which made a significant contribution to the study of crowd psychology.[2]

❝ There was scarcely any question of the peasants before July 14. Yet they formed at least three quarters of the population of the kingdom and we realize today that without their adherence the Revolution could with difficulty have succeeded. ... The peasant uprising is one of the most distinctive features of the Revolution in France. **❞**

Georges Lefebvre, *The Coming of the French Revolution*

In the same year Lefebvre published a lesser-known piece, *Questions Agraires au Temps de la Terreur* (Agrarian Questions at the Time of the Terror), which demonstrated how problems with food supply were central to the demand for vengeance against perceived enemies.[3] In 1935 Lefebvre wrote a history of Napoleon,* the Corsican-born general who became the emperor of France. A biography might seem an unusual project for a social historian, but Lefebvre wanted to focus on the social situation that Napoleon emerged from. The man was shown to reflect the "temperament" of his era.[4] Lefebvre believed that it was the bourgeoisie* who allowed Napoleon to introduce his military dictatorship in 1799, because they wanted him to protect the legal and property gains they had made in 1789.[5]

The Coming of the French Revolution, written in 1939, contained several echoes of these earlier works. It also highlighted the role of the masses, rather than individuals, in making history and examined the relation between economic and political change. In *The Coming of the French Revolution* Lefebvre also revealed his fascination with what happens to people's psychologies when they are acting together, exposing "the deeper workings of the peasant mind" and the "passionate feelings, the fear, the frenzy for fighting, the thirst for revenge that characterized the days of July."[6] After World War II,*

Lefebvre wrote a number of far-ranging analyses of the revolution from 1789 to 1799.[7] Although broad in scope and compellingly written, these grand overviews lack the originality of Lefebvre's pre-war publications, which remain the most enduring part of his body of work.

Integration

The most original and important contribution Lefebvre made to the study of the French Revolution was his close study of the rural environment. Like fellow historians Albert Mathiez* and Ernest Labrousse,* he recognized that changes in the supply of grain for food could have dramatic effects on political behavior. Yet by making the peasants the center of his analysis he was going beyond both Jacobin* and Marxist* traditions. Jacobins tended to emphasize the unity of *le peuple* (the people) in bringing about change, overlooking the large differences between urban and rural worlds. Marxists, on the other hand, tended to see the proletariat*—the industrial working classes— as the most important people in bringing about change.

There had been a spontaneous peasant revolution in 1789, Lefebvre argues, even if it was an unconventional one. The peasants did not wait for a sign from the cities to revolt; they set about taking their "cause into their own hands and delivering a death blow to what was left of the feudal* and manorial system."*[8]

This desire to demonstrate the independent actions of the peasantry was an important part of Lefebvre's socialist* politics. But it also reflected his faith in scientific, social history. "For the last half century," Lefebvre wrote appreciatively, "students have applied themselves, and rightly so, to the task of showing how the revolutionary spirit originated in a social and economic movement."[9] In his later works Lefebvre continued to see the peasantry as having played a central role in the revolution and its aftermath. The revolutionary government failed to deal with rural grievances. The unpopular conscription into the army and the slaughter of many peasants during the Terror* further alienated the rural poor.[10] The problems that existed between the peasants and the Jacobins* in charge had a negative impact on the success of the revolution as a whole.

Significance

Thanks to its translation in 1947 by Robert R. Palmer, *The Coming of the French Revolution* remains Lefebvre's most famous work outside of France. The book sold forty thousand copies in English before the author's death in 1959 and it became required reading at university campuses throughout Britain and the United States.[11] Although historians might have more respect for *The Great Fear* on the grounds of its innovative methods, this text was not used in the classroom. By contrast, *The Coming of the French Revolution* was the definitive book about the social origins of the revolution, bringing together the latest findings into a readable narrative. As the British historian Norman Hampson* remarked: "The debate on the French Revolution seemed to have reached a conclusion and there was something so splendidly definitive about Lefebvre's *Coming of the French Revolution* that few were disposed to express any doubts about the quality of the emperor's tailoring."[12]

The book was much less important in France, where it was only republished by Lefebvre's own student Albert Soboul* in 1970. Lefebvre had been reluctant to generalize and had always been sensitive to the complexity of the data on which he based his opinions. But his followers stated much more bluntly that the revolution had been caused by the emergence of the bourgeoisie,* who oversaw the transition from feudal to capitalist* systems of production. As Soboul declared in 1953, the French Revolution represented "the culmination of a long economic and social evolution that made the bourgeoisie the mistress of the world," after dispatching "a decadent aristocracy holding tenaciously to its privileges."[13]

A new crop of historians, however, attacked such views, believing them to be stated with a misplaced confidence.

NOTES

1   Georges Lefebvre, *La Grande Peur de 1789* (Paris: Armand Colin, 1932).

2   Georges Lefebvre, "Les Foules révolutionnaires," in *La Foule: Quatrième semaine internationale de synthèse*, ed. Paul Alphandéry et al. (Paris: Felix Alcan, 1934), 79–107.

3   Lefebvre, *Questions agraires au temps de la Terreur* (Strasbourg: Lening, 1932).

4   Georges Lefebvre, *Napoléon* (Paris: Felix Alcan, 1935).

5   Georges Lefebvre, *The Coming of the French Revolution*, trans. Robert R. Palmer (Princeton, NJ: Princeton University Press, 2005), 212.

6   Lefebvre, *The Coming of the French Revolution*, 140, 210.

7   Georges Lefebvre, *Le Directoire* (Paris: Armand Colin, 1946). Georges Lefebvre, *La Révolution française* (Paris: Presses Universitaires de France, 1951).

8   Lefebvre, *The Coming of the French Revolution*, 129.

9   Lefebvre, *The Coming of the French Revolution*, 48.

10 Georges Lefebvre, Études orléanaises: Contribution à l'étude des structures sociales à la fin du XVIIIe siècle, 2 vols. (Paris: Commission d'histoire économique et sociale de la Révolution française, 1962–3).

11 Beatrice Hyslop, "Georges Lefebvre, Historian," in *French Historical Studies* 1 (1960).

12 Norman Hampson, "The French Revolution and its Historians," in *The Permanent Revolution*, ed. Geoffrey Best (London: Fontana, 1988), 43.

13 Albert Soboul, "Classes and Class Struggles during the French Revolution," *Science and Society* 17 (1953): 238, 245.

SECTION 3
IMPACT

MODULE 9
THE FIRST RESPONSES

KEY POINTS

- In the 1950s and 1960s, the historians Alfred Cobban* and George V. Taylor* attacked Lefebvre's ideas, reviving the view that the origins of the French Revolution* lay in politics, not social conflict, as the Marxist* interpretation had it.

- Lefebvre condemned Cobban's views as a typical example of British conservatism,* which threatened to rob the revolution of its meaning.

- The view was put forward that the French Revolution was not a social revolution with political consequences, as Lefebvre argued, but rather a political revolution with social consequences.

Criticism

In 1955 the first significant criticism was leveled against Georges Lefebvre's *The Coming of the French Revolution.* It was delivered by Albert Cobban, a newly appointed professor at the University of London, in a lecture titled "The Myth of the French Revolution."[1] Cobban said it was simply not true that the French Revolution replaced a feudal* system of landowners and dependent peasants with a capitalist* system dominated by the bourgeoisie.* He argued that eighteenth-century France was not feudal. It was a buoyant commercial society where many of the old aristocratic* privileges had already disappeared.

Cobban also looked at the capitalist credentials of the group that Lefebvre called the bourgeoisie. The Marxist labels that Lefebvre had used to define his social groups suggested that the bourgeoisie should possess commercial or industrial wealth. Cobban looked at the backgrounds of the men who had been elected to represent the "Third

❝ To pass from the general to the particular, in the French Revolution, it is commonly said, the feudal order passed away and the rule of the bourgeoisie took its place. This is, put simply, the myth which has dominated serious research on the history of the French Revolution during the present century. **❞**

Alfred Cobban, "The Myth of the French Revolution"

Estate"* (that is, the common people) at the Estates General* (a national assembly convened in 1789 for the first time since 1614). Cobban found that only 13% were linked to commerce, while nearly 70% were lawyers. Even more tellingly, around 43% of the bourgeois deputies* were holders of low-ranking positions of office. They had profited from the royal policy of venality,* the selling off of positions in administration, such as the job of tax collector, in order to raise funds. This led Cobban to claim that the bourgeoisie had little hatred for "feudal" privilege and that they had in fact greedily acquired these privileges for themselves whenever they were up for sale.

Cobban did not doubt that the events of 1789 had their social and economic causes. He also thought that Lefebvre and his disciples had put forward the wrong economic explanation. This is why his critique is sometimes called "soft revisionism."* Cobban argued that the bourgeoisie were not in the forefront of a new, thrusting capitalist class; for him, they rebelled against the crown because their finances were declining and their position was becoming more precarious.[2]

Responses

Lefebvre published a fiery response to Cobban in the *Historical Annals of the French Revolution*, the journal he had edited for nearly 30 years. Cobban had missed the point of his work, he said, and taking issue with the term "feudal" was just quibbling about terminology. Whether or not the representatives of the Third Estate were capitalists themselves was not really important. The point was that, by sweeping away inherited privilege, the French Revolution helped to transform France into a capitalist society.

Further, Lefebvre argued, Cobban was attempting to minimize the importance of 1789 in order to show that violent revolution was wrong. He was not surprised that an English historian would try to do this; England was a deeply conservative country, he thought.[3] These quite bitter exchanges were further inflamed by the fact that the Cold War* was in full flow. Many academic debates at the time were shaped by the broader rivalry between capitalism and communism.*

Although Lefebvre died in 1959, his followers took up the battle with Cobban. In 1964 Cobban published *The Social Interpretation of the French Revolution*, in which he repeated his criticism of Lefebvre's theories, arguing that "so far as capitalist economic developments were at issue, it was a Revolution not for, but against, capitalism." That this fact had been obscured for so long was the fault of Marxist assumptions, "an un-historical sociological theory."[4]

The final chapter of Cobban's book once again turned Lefebvre's own evidence against him. Cobban argued that the materials published posthumously in Lefebvre's final book, Études orléanaises (Orleanist Studies) had more in common with Cobban's own views than with Lefebvre's.[5]

A fierce back-and-forth battle took place between the historian Jacques Godechot* and Cobban, while the *Historical Annals of the French Revolution* decided not even to review Cobban's book.[6] In contrast to the close relationship between Lefebvre and his translator Robert R. Palmer,* French and Anglo-American scholarship had begun to split into hostile camps.

Conflict and Consensus

In 1964 the American doctoral student George V. Taylor* published research that supported Cobban's argument. Taylor had been studying the types of capitalism that had existed in pre-revolutionary France, and arguing that the country's growing industries were dominated by the nobility.[7] In 1967 he added that most forms of wealth in the eighteenth century had been based on ownership of property, because a person's capital was overwhelmingly tied up in land.[8] Taken together, these conclusions suggested that the growth of capitalism was only a minor cause of the French Revolution.

Lefebvre's characterization of the different social classes was starting to disintegrate under pressure. The social historian Robert Forster* demonstrated that the French nobility were not people trying to manage their debts, but were rather shrewd and frugal managers of their estates.[9] The British historian C. B. A. Behrens,* meanwhile, found that French nobles were much more highly taxed than their European equivalents. The major beneficiaries of tax exemption were not the nobility, but in fact the commercial bourgeoisie.[10] Additionally, Enlightenment* ideas, which Lefebvre had associated with the bourgeoisie, were talked about more regularly by the nobles than by the members of the Third Estate (that is, the common people).[11]

In *The Coming of the French Revolution*, Lefebvre had treated the aristocracy and the bourgeoisie as separate groups, hostile to each other. Within a few years of his death, several American scholars noted that tensions seemed to exist *within* social classes (rich nobles against poor nobles), rather than *between* social classes. George V. Taylor went beyond the "soft revisionism" of Cobban to embrace a "hard revisionism" that cast doubt on every aspect of the social interpretation favored by Lefebvre. Class conflict, it now seemed, was not the main reason behind the French Revolution. For Taylor, 1789 was "essentially a political Revolution with social consequences and not a social Revolution with political consequences."[12]

NOTES

1   Alfred Cobban, *Aspects of the French Revolution* (London: Jonathan Cape, 1968), 90–112.

2   Cobban, *Aspects of the French Revolution*, 90–112.

3   Georges Lefebvre, "The Myth of the French Revolution," *Annales historiques de la Révolution française* 28 (1956).

4   Alfred Cobban, *The Social Interpretation of the French Revolution* (Cambridge: Cambridge University Press, 1964), 172–3.

5   Georges Lefebvre, Études orléanaises: Contribution à l'étude des structures sociales à la fin du XVIIIᵉ siècle, 2 vols. (Paris: Commission d'histoire économique et sociale de la Révolution française, 1962–3).

6   Jacques Godechot, "The Social Interpretation of the French Revolution," *Revue Historique* 235 (1966). Cobban, *Aspects of the French Revolution*, 264–87. Godechot made no mention of Cobban or Taylor in his survey of revolutionary historiography. Jacques Godechot, *Un Jury pour la Révolution* (Paris: Robert Laffont, 1974).

7   George V. Taylor, "Types of Capitalism in Eighteenth-Century France," *English Historical Review* 79 (1964).

8   George V. Taylor, "Noncapitalist Wealth and the Origins of the French Revolution," *American Historical Review* 72 (1967).

9   Robert Forster, *The Nobility of Toulouse in the Eighteenth Century: A Social and Economic Study* (Baltimore: Johns Hopkins University Press, 1960).

10 C. B. A. Behrens, "Nobles, Privileges and Taxes in France at the end of the Ancien Regime," *Economic History Review* 15 (1962–3).

11 Guy Chaussinand-Nogaret, *La Noblesse au XVIIIᵉ siècle: De la féodalité aux lumières* (Paris: Hachette, 1976).

12 Taylor, "Noncapitalist Wealth," 491.

MODULE 10
THE EVOLVING DEBATE

KEY POINTS

- Many Anglo-American historians prefer to think of the French Revolution* as a product of developing political ideas and cultural struggles.

- Some scholars now think that the peasants' fight for their rights was a battle that had been brewing for many years before the revolution—and it continued afterwards, too.

- Scholars who took another look at the French Revolution disagreed with Lefebvre's view that there were different classes with different agendas. They downplayed long-term issues in favor of looking at how short-term triggers caused the revolution.

Uses and Problems

From the 1960s, British and American scholars have questioned the social origins of the revolution. In many cases, the revisionists* did not say that Georges Lefebvre's data was incorrect, but they did show that it could be interpreted in a non–Marxist* way. Some disputed Lefebvre's Marx-inspired vision of four social classes, for instance. The historian François Furet,* however, went further. A former communist,* Furet launched a withering attack on Marxist historians for treating the revolution as "orthodoxy."[1] Furet used religious comparisons to put forward the view that Marxists ignored evidence simply so they could keep believing that the revolution had social origins.

Rather than look to Marx,* Furet revisited the ideas of the statesman and historian Alexis de Tocqueville,* whose *L'Ancien Régime et la Révolution* (The Old Regime and the Revolution, 1856) identified how there was a clear relationship between the centralizing of political

> **66** [Essentially] a political Revolution with social consequences and not a social Revolution with political consequences. **99**
>
> George V. Taylor, "Noncapitalist Wealth and the Origins of the French Revolution"

power under the monarchy* and the growing power of the state under the Jacobins* (an important faction in the post-revolution political environment and government) and Napoleon,* a charismatic military leader who seized power in 1799. [2]

In *Interpreting the French Revolution* (1978), Furet lambasted Lefebvre for continuing to believe that the revolution marked the start of the modern world.[3] Following Tocqueville, Furet insisted that the revolution did not represent a clean break with the past. Instead it merely accelerated processes that were already happening in eighteenth-century France. The only area where things were markedly different was in the ways people talked and thought about politics. For Furet, these new political languages were the central achievement of the revolution. He accused social historians like Lefebvre of naivety in simply repeating the views of the revolutionaries themselves, and asserting that the world after 1789 was "a time both qualitatively new and different."[4] In reality, things changed only slowly. What mattered was that the revolutionaries *believed* that total change was possible. Following Furet's lead, most historians of the revolution today look at the origins of 1789 by studying these "utopian" political languages and political culture.[5]

Schools of Thought

Lefebvre's way of thinking was still admired by those who liked to look at "history from below"* in the 1950s and 1960s. His emphasis on the importance of the general population in the French

Revolution was crucial to Albert Soboul's* classic 1958 study of the *sans-culottes*,* those who were fighting for social equality in the aftermath of 1789. It was also important to George Rudé's* research into the revolutionary crowd, and Richard Cobb's* study of the revolutionary armies that carried out many of the violent acts associated with the Terror.*[6]

These historians tried to marry an analysis of statistical data with an insight into what people were generally thinking at the time, and paid a great deal of attention to Lefebvre's groundbreaking article of 1934 on the revolutionary crowds.[7] Lefebvre's successor at the Sorbonne,* the historian Michel Vovelle,* has continued Lefebvre's mixing of methods from Marxism and the *Annales** school to better understand popular mindsets and mentalities.[8]

In recent years, doubts have been voiced about parts of Lefebvre's interpretation of peasant politics.[9] For instance, the Great Fear*—the panic among peasants that there was a deliberate conspiracy in 1789 to starve them into submission—was not just hostile to the aristocracy,* but also targeted tax collectors, royal officials, and wealthy townsmen. It was also restricted primarily to the region around Paris.[10] Yet the foremost experts on the peasantry have continued to defend Lefebvre's insight that the peasants were acting on their own initiative, springing into action even before the opening meeting of the Estates General* in May 1789.[11] The American sociologist John Markoff * has built on Lefebvre's work to offer a wider chronology of how the peasants overthrew feudalism. Many of the laws that allowed this to happen did not come into effect until much later. Markoff has highlighted the peasants' drawn-out and violent struggle to win the freedoms that were promised in 1789.[12]

In Current Scholarship

Following the revisionist* trend of the 1960s, the references to class conflict in *The Coming of the French Revolution* made the book seem dated. As the Soviet Union* began to fail, and the theoretical foundations of communism began to be questioned, any book with the bourgeoisie at its center was seen to be "gloriously *depassé*" (old fashioned).[13] Although it should be noted that most of the revisionists' criticisms were aimed not at Lefebvre but at his more dogmatic pupil, Albert Soboul, Lefebvre and his followers were lumped together into a single unloved Marxist school. The American professor Marvin Cox* has protested at how misleading this "Marxist" label can be, pointing out that Lefebvre was also considered an early revisionist when he died in 1959; he was, after all, testing and transforming the models he had received from the socialist leader Jean Jaurès* and the historian Albert Mathiez* before him.[14]

By the end of the 1970s, the Marxist vision of the French Revolution was no longer seen as credible. William Doyle's* classic revisionist text, *The Origins of the French Revolution* (1980), was a clear attempt to displace Lefebvre's book as the definitive new version of what happened in 1789. Lefebvre's concern with social factors was replaced with a firm emphasis on the crucial importance of politics and the key role of accidental happenings.[15] In its skepticism towards all social explanations of the French Revolution, Doyle's book defined the mood of "hard revisionism."

Following the attack on Lefebvre's work by Furet, many historians in the 1980s and 1990s switched their attention to the study of political language and, especially, political culture. Furet's approach was a major influence on American historians such as Keith Baker* and Lynn Hunt.*[16] His understanding of 1789 was the most widely read and debated in France at the time of the bicentenary* celebrations of the revolution in 1989.[17]

NOTES

1   François Furet, "Sur le catéchisme de la Révolution française," *Annales: économies, sociétés, civilisations* 26, no. 2 (1971).

2   Alexis de Tocqueville, *L'Ancien Régime et la Révolution* (Paris, 1856).

3   François Furet, "The French Revolution is Over, " in *Interpreting the French Revolution* (Cambridge: Cambridge University Press, 1981), 1–79.

4   Furet referred in particular to Lefebvre's essay, "La Révolution française et les paysans", in Georges Lefebvre, Études sur la Révolution française (Paris: Presses Universitaires de France, 1954), 246–68.

5   See Keith Michael Baker, *Inventing the French Revolution: Essays on French Political Culture in the Eighteenth Century* (Cambridge: Cambridge University Press, 1990).

6   Albert Soboul, *Les Sans-culottes parisiens en l'an II: Mouvement populaire et gouvernement révolutionnaire, 2 juin 1793–9 thermidor an II* (Paris: Clavreuil, 1958); George Rudé, *The Crowd in the French Revolution* (Oxford: Oxford University Press, 1959); Richard Cobb, *Les Armées révolutionnaires: Instrument de la Terreur dans les départements, avril 1793–floréal an II*, 2 vols. (Paris: Mouton, 1961–3).

7   Georges Lefebvre, "Les Foules révolutionnaires," in *La Foule: Quatrième semaine internationale de synthèse*, ed. Paul Alphandéry et al. (Paris: Felix Alcan, 1934), 79–107.

8   Michel Vovelle, *La Mentalité révolutionnaire: Société et mentalités sous la Révolution française (1789–1989)* (Paris: Éditions Sociales, 1985).

9   Hilton Root, "The Case against Georges Lefebvre's Peasant Revolution," *History Workshop Journal* 28 (1989).

10 Timothy Tackett, "Collective Panics in the early French Revolution, 1789–1791: A Comparative Perspective," *French History* 17 (2003).

11 Peter M. Jones, "Georges Lefebvre and the Peasant Revolution: Fifty Years On," *French Historical Studies* 16 (1990). See also Peter M. Jones, *The Peasantry in the French Revolution* (Cambridge: Cambridge University Press, 1988).

12 John Markoff, "Violence, Emancipation, and Democracy: The Countryside and the French Revolution," *American Historical Review* 100 (1995); John Markoff, *The Abolition of Feudalism: Peasants, Lords and Legislators in the French Revolution* (University Park: Pennsylvania State University Press, 1996).

13 Colin Jones, "Bourgeois Revolution Revivified: 1789 and Social Change," in *Rewriting the French Revolution*, ed. Colin Lucas (Oxford: Oxford University Press, 1991), 71.

14 Marvin Cox, "Furet, Cobban, Marx: The Revision of the 'Orthodoxy' Revisited," *Historical Reflections* 27, no. 1 (2001).

15 William Doyle, *Origins of the French Revolution* (Oxford: Oxford University Press, 1980).

16 Baker, *Inventing the French Revolution*; Lynn Hunt, *Politics, Culture and Class in the French Revolution* (Berkeley: University of California Press, 1984).

17 Stephen J. Kaplan, *Farewell Revolution: Disputed Legacies—France 1789/1989* (Ithaca, NY: Cornell University Press, 1995).

MODULE 11
IMPACT AND INFLUENCE TODAY

KEY POINTS

• There is currently a new desire to find a middle ground between Marxist* and revisionist* approaches to the French Revolution*—that is, roughly, to find an interpretation that accounts for both politics and tensions between social classes.

• Many scholars now accept that social differences did influence the way in which politics worked in eighteenth-century France.

• There has been more study of the parts played in the French Revolution by consumerism,* civic identities, and women.

Position

Georges Lefebvre's *The Coming of the French Revolution* continues to hold a place in scholarship of the French Revolution.

Following the bicentenary* in 1989 (the 200th anniversary of the revolution) and the end of the Cold War,* the gap between Marxist and revisionist historians has started to close. The British history professor Gwynne Lewis* observed that a commitment to social history does not mean you have to use Marxist categories. She called on historians on both sides to acknowledge that it was "the involvement of peasants, artisans and shopkeepers which provided the main dynamic of the Revolution during its early years."[1] Under the influence of revisionism, historians were led to the study of politics and political languages. As a consequence, they ended up studying elite groups who had power and were politically eloquent. Recently there has been a call for a return to studying how the revolution

> **66** [The] definition of the revolution as politics, and of politics as the attempt to speak from a position of sovereignty, freed historians of any need to think about all the people who never came near that position. **99**
>
> Rebecca Spang, "Paradigms and Paranoia: How Modern is the French Revolution?"

touched the everyday lives of ordinary citizens.[2] This has been coupled with a deeper study of revolutionary institutions themselves, judging the French Revolution by what it actually achieved rather than by what its leaders wrote and said.[3]

These explanations have included some of the themes that *The Coming of the French Revolution* did not address. Traditional social history was undoubtedly highly male-oriented, and Lefebvre did not pay enough attention to the role of revolutionary women. Research has since shown the extent to which women made their own decisions to revolt in 1789, especially during the October Days* when groups of women marched to the palace of Versailles* to demand bread from the king.[4]

Lefebvre's faith in the Declaration of the Rights of Man,* and the fact that these rights belonged to all humanity, encouraged him to think that over time the revolutionaries would have been able to give these rights to both women and slaves in the colonies.[5] However, although histories placing the revolution in relation to gender politics and empire studies have flourished,[6] many feminists have seen all talk of "the rights of man" as excluding women, because the freedom of men depended on keeping women in the home.[7]

Interaction

Dissatisfied with the alternative explanations of the revisionists, some historians are rethinking class differences in the eighteenth century. In the early 1990s the British historian Colin Jones* published an article called "Bourgeois Revolution Revivified," in which he claims Lefebvre was right to see the eighteenth century as a time of profound social and economic change. There was, he argues, a clear increase in demand for consumer goods produced by more commercial activity. This boom in consumerism led to the emergence of a group of market-orientated, liberal professionals who cared about the general wellbeing of the people. It was this group that predominated among the deputies* in the Third Estate* (representatives of the common people), and which would come to shape the laws introduced by the new National Assembly* that abolished guilds and removed hereditary privilege.[8] The battle over the bourgeois* *causes* of the French Revolution might have been lost, but the battle over its bourgeois *consequences* has not. This can be seen most clearly in the growing interest in money and markets during the revolutionary period.[9]

Coming from a different perspective, the American historian William Sewell* has shown a way of bridging the old social history and the revisionist interest in political ideas. In his 1789 analysis of Abbé Sieyès's* *Qu'est-ce que le Tiers État?* (What is the Third Estate?), Sewell shows the text to be full of ideas about class. Sieyès used economic analysis to denounce the luxuries enjoyed by the old aristocracy* and to celebrate a new class of rational and productive professional men who could govern over the workers. These ideas had a direct influence on policies decided by the National Assembly in the years immediately following the revolution.[10] By contrast, the American historian Sarah Maza* has insisted that class needs to be approached less as a social fact than as a vocabulary for describing society. Rather than ditch the terminology of social class, modern scholars are more inclined to explore how it was culturally reimagined across the revolutionary era.[11]

The Continuing Debate

Carla Hesse* of the University of California has recently claimed that a new middle ground between Marxists and revisionists has emerged, occupied by a group she calls "new Jacobins."*[12] Hesse stresses the new wave of interest in understanding how the institutions of the monarchy* actually worked. Although there might be disagreement about the role of social class, there is agreement that the main reason why the king found himself vulnerable was the dire financial situation the country found itself in. A host of new studies have appeared on royal finances which show how much the health of the kingdom's finances depended not just on international bankers, but also on trade within the French colonial empire.[13] So to some degree the causes of the French Revolution no longer seem to lie just within France itself.

Although social history is returning to favor, few scholars today would agree with the view that the revolution was a key moment in the history of capitalism,* or that it was led by an ambitious bourgeoisie. Many historians still believe that there must be some link between social conditions and political action. The American historian Timothy Tackett's* work on the deputies of the National Assembly, for instance, showed that there were still major differences between former nobles and commoners.[14] It is clear that there were strong connections between certain middling professions and revolutionary activism, and that the courtroom and the pulpit could provide excellent training grounds for learning how to appeal to public opinion.[15]

Yet the revisionist position of the former Marxist historian François Furet, a scholar thoroughly engaged in the discussion of political ideology, often far removed from any practical context, is also being modified. Political historians today are much more likely to study the actual daily business of politics, including the very real threats of force or royal counterattack that haunted the revolutionaries.[16] The more the scholarship has developed, the more it has become clear that the causes of the revolution were many, complex, and overlapping.

NOTES

1 Gwynne Lewis, *The French Revolution: Rethinking the Debate* (London: Routledge, 1993), 122.

2 Peter McPhee, *Living the French Revolution, 1789–99* (Basingstoke: Palgrave Macmillan, 2009).

3 Isser Woloch, *The New Regime: Transformations of the French Civic Order, 1789–1920s* (New York: Norton, 1995).

4 Olwen Hufton, *Women and the Limits of Citizenship in the French Revolution* (Toronto: University of Toronto Press, 1992).

5 Georges Lefebvre, *The Coming of the French Revolution*, trans. Robert R. Palmer (Princeton, NJ: Princeton University Press, 2005), 208.

6 Lynn Hunt, Suzanne Desan, and William Nelson (eds.), *The French Revolution in Global Perspective* (Ithaca, NY: Cornell University Press, 2013); Bailey Stone, *Reinterpreting the French Revolution: A Global-Historical Perspective* (Cambridge: Cambridge University Press, 2002); Suzanne Desan, *The Family on Trial in Revolutionary France* (Berkeley: University of California Press, 2004).

7 Joan Scott, *Only Paradoxes to Offer: French Feminists and the Rights of Man* (Cambridge, MA: Harvard University Press, 1996).

8 Colin Jones, "Bourgeois Revolution Revivified: 1789 and Social Change," in *Rewriting the French Revolution*, ed. Colin Lucas (Oxford: Clarendon Press, 1991), 113–14.

9 William Reddy, *Money and Liberty in Western Europe: A Critique of Historical Understanding* (Cambridge: Cambridge University Press, 1987), 107–53.

10 William H. Sewell, Jr., *A Rhetoric of Bourgeois Revolution: The abbé Sièyes and What is the Third Estate?* (Durham, NC: Duke University Press, 1994).

11 Sarah Maza, *The Myth of the French Bourgeoisie: An Essay in the Social Imaginary, 1750–1850* (Cambridge, MA: Harvard University Press, 2003).

12 Carla Hesse, "The New Jacobins," *French Historical Studies* 32, no. 4 (2009).

13 John Shovlin, *The Political Economy of Virtue: Luxury, Patriotism and the Origins of the French Revolution* (Ithaca, NY: Cornell University Press, 2006); Michael Kwass, *Privilege and the Politics of Taxation in Eighteenth-Century France: Liberté, Égalité, Fiscalité* (Cambridge: Cambridge University Press, 2000); Michael Sonenscher, *Before the Deluge: Public Debt, Inequality and the Intellectual Origins of the French Revolution* (Princeton, NJ: Princeton University Press, 2007).

14 Timothy Tackett, "Nobles and Third Estate in the Revolutionary Dynamic of the National Assembly, 1789–90," *American Historical Review* 94 (1989).

15 Michael Sonenscher, *Work and Wages: Natural Law, Politics, and Eighteenth-Century France* (Cambridge: Cambridge University Press, 1989); Colin Jones, *The Charitable Imperative: Hospitals and Nursing in Ancien Regime and Revolutionary France* (London: Routledge, 1989); Sarah Maza, *Private Lives and Public Affairs: The Causes Celebres of Prerevolutionary France* (Berkeley and London: University of California Press, 1993).

16 Munro Price, *The Fall of the French Monarchy: Louis XVI, Marie Antoinette and the Baron de Breteuil* (London: Palgrave Macmillan, 2002).

WHERE NEXT?

KEY POINTS

- *The Coming of the French Revolution* remains a subtle, approachable distillation of the Marxist* tradition in revolutionary history writing.

- The text will continue to inspire those who study "history from below,"* offering accounts that emphasize the historical role, concerns, and worldview of people outside the social and political elite—historians, that is, who believe that political conflicts often have social origins.

- Lefebvre was a fervent republican* and patriot writing at a time of peril, with Europe under threat from the Nazis.* His work was both a celebration of the French Revolution* and a call to arms to defend its legacy.

Potential

Although more than 70 years have passed since Georges Lefebvre's *The Coming of the French Revolution* was published, it remains an indispensable book on the origins of the French Revolution. Its insights into French society in the eighteenth century continue to inspire scholars working in the field of "history from below." It remains a useful overview of what happened in 1789, and Lefebvre's intelligent discussion of the many factors that produced the revolution continues to provoke debate and stimulate research.

In a 2005 edition, the historian Timothy Tackett* applauds Lefebvre for producing a "masterpiece of narrative and analytical concision" that vividly brings the era and its passions to life, and that joins the ranks of Jules Michelet,* Alexis de Tocqueville* and Jean Jaurès* as "one of the great classics of French Revolutionary history."[1]

> ❝ Liberty is by no means an invitation to indifference or to irresponsible power; nor is it the promise of unlimited well-being without a counterpart of toil and effort. It supposes application, perpetual effort, strict government of self, sacrifice in contingencies, civic and private virtues. It is therefore more difficult to live as a free man than to live as a slave, and that is why men so often renounce their freedom; for freedom is in its way an invitation, and sometimes of heroism, as the freedom of the Christian is an invitation to a life of sainthood. ❞
>
> Georges Lefebvre, *The Coming of the French Revolution*

All scholars who still believe in some kind of social interpretation of the events of 1789—even if it is no longer a Marxist interpretation—will admire Lefebvre and will need to take on his works.

Lefebvre's single, synthetic interpretation of the events of 1789 continues to appeal. The historian François Furet* tried to produce another interpretation, but many scholars are unconvinced by his dismissal of all kinds of social factors in the story of the French Revolution.[2] Similarly, the historian William Doyle* gave an excellent insight into high politics in *The Origins of the French Revolution* but did not bring together the concerns of the elite with those of the masses.[3] While the British social historian Simon Schama's* *Citizens* suffers from its suggestion that the revolution was always destined to end in disaster.[4] There is no longer one view that seems adequate to explain how and why the French Revolution occurred and, for this reason, the challenge of creating the defining text about the revolution remains.

Future Directions

It could be argued that the revisionists* won: no scholar today would argue for a "bourgeois* revolution" with the same confidence as

Lefebvre or his student, Albert Soboul.* Nor would they support Lefebvre's claim that the Enlightenment* marked the victory of "bourgeois" ideals or that each social class had a clearly defined plan as to how they were going to achieve their goals.[5] In 1787 the nobility was leading opposition to the king. Yet in July 1790 it was abolished as a hereditary class. The work of the revisionists has shown that Lefebvre's claim of a single "aristocratic reaction"* in the eighteenth century is simplistic.[6] For modern social historians the picture presented in *The Coming of the French Revolution* is just too neat and tidy.

Many social historians are, nevertheless, dissatisfied with claims that reduce what happened in 1789 to nothing more than some short-term blunders or some long-term political trends. The former cannot explain how ordinary people organized and managed to influence history in such a profound way. The latter explanations struggle to account for the precise timing of the crisis. Why was it in 1789 that the monarchy* fell, and not in any previous year? The appeal of Lefebvre's account comes from his openness to all kinds of different explanations of events. What cannot be denied is that in 1789 "the economic and political crises came together in their effects."[7]

The latest champions of the social interpretation of the 1789 show their loyalty to Lefebvre's complex arguments. While the statistics relating to contemporary prices provided by the economic historian Ernest Labrousse* have been disputed, there is clear evidence that late eighteenth-century France was coping with population pressures, rapid urbanization, surging inflation and an over-taxed agricultural sector. Rather than make sweeping generalizations, modern historians would stress the contrasts between prosperity and hardship *within* each class. "These problems and divisions by themselves did not cause the Revolution," wrote the sociologist and political scientist Jack Goldstone in 2011. "But they created obstacles to reform and gave rise to material grievances that helped motivate actions guided by the ideological and cultural shifts of the day."[8]

Summary

The Coming of the French Revolution remains an indispensable book about the French Revolution. The shrewd balance of detailed historical evidence and passionate personal commitment from its author shows not just why the French Revolution broke out, but why it still matters two centuries later. The appeal of Lefebvre's account came from his interest in the large number of factors that led to the revolution, taking into account the actions of the masses as well as the actions of the elite. The complex notion of four interconnected but independent revolutions happening at the same time explained why even the men who thought they were its leaders in 1789 soon found events spinning out of their control. Even revisionist historians who disagreed with Lefebvre, such as William Doyle, acknowledged that *The Coming of the French Revolution* was "subtle and skillfully written," and could not be easily summarized. "To appreciate its full flavor there is no substitute for reading the book itself."[9]

Those aspects of Lefebvre's ideas about class relations that were considered less convincing came under heavy attack from revisionists in the 1960s and 1970s. However, Lefebvre's emphasis on the way that political, ideological, and economic factors all came together to ignite popular protest was still inspirational. His work will continue to invite further research.

The Coming of the French Revolution is also an idealistic book. In recent years historians have focused on the dark side of the revolutionaries, their intolerance towards perceived enemies such as traitorous aristocrats,* renegade priests, conquered populations, colonial slaves or even "irrational" women.[10] Writing at a time when the French Republic's founding values were in danger—the German occupation of World War II*—Lefebvre chose to celebrate the achievements of 1789. He believed that by teaching his fellow citizens the origins of the French

Revolution, and what it was fighting against, he could also help people in the future to achieve some of its unfulfilled aspirations.

NOTES

1   Timothy Tackett, "Introduction," in Georges Lefebvre, *The Coming of the French Revolution* (Princeton, NJ: Princeton University Press, 2005), xxx.

2   François Furet, *La Révolution: De Turgot à Jules Ferry, 1770–1880* (Paris: Hachette, 1988).

3   William Doyle, *Origins of the French Revolution* (Oxford: Oxford University Press, 1980).

4   Simon Schama, *Citizens: A Chronicle of the French Revolution* (London: Penguin, 1989).

5   Dan Edelmann, *The Enlightenment: A Genealogy* (Chicago: University of Chicago Press, 2010).

6   William Doyle, *Aristocracy and its Enemies in the Age of Revolution* (Oxford: Oxford University Press, 2009).

7   Georges Lefebvre, *The Coming of the French Revolution*, trans. Robert R. Palmer (Princeton, NJ: Princeton University Press, 2005), 195.

8   Jack A. Goldstone, "The Social Origins of the French Revolution Revisited," in From *Deficit to Deluge: The Origins of the French Revolution*, ed. Dale Van Kley and Thomas E. Kaiser (Stanford, CA: Stanford University Press, 2011), 103.

9   Doyle, *Origins of the French Revolution*, 3.

10 For a sample of this literature, see Patrice Higonnet, *Goodness Beyond Virtue: Jacobins during the French Revolution* (Cambridge, MA: Harvard University Press, 1998); Nigel Aston, *Religion and Revolution in France, 1780–1804* (Basingstoke: Macmillan, 2000); T. C. W. Blanning, *The French Revolution in Germany: Occupation and Resistance in the Rhineland, 1792–1802* (Oxford: Clarendon Press, 1983); Olwen Hufton, *Women and the Limits of Citizenship in the French Revolution* (Toronto: University of Toronto Press, 1992); and Laurent Dubois, *A Colony of Citizens: Revolution and Slave Emancipation in the French Caribbean, 1787–1804* (Chapel Hill: University of North Carolina Press, 2004).

GLOSSARY

GLOSSARY OF TERMS

Absolutism: a mode of governance that emerged in the monarchies of seventeenth- and eighteenth-century Europe, stressing the sovereign as the source of all authority. In France it reached its peak under Louis XIV, the king on the throne at the time of the French Revolution.

Action Française: a French monarchist association, founded in 1898, defined by its anti-republican, anti-Semitic, counterrevolutionary, and profoundly nationalist views. Shaped by the doctrines of Charles Maurras, it attained maximum influence after World War I, and welcomed the Vichy government.

American Revolution: the uprising by the colonists of America against the British government, which led to the American War of Independence (1776–83) and the creation of the United States.

Annales **school:** the most important movement in twentieth-century French historiography, recognized for its pioneering interest in quantitative history (research conducted through the study of statistics, for example), the social sciences, and comparative history. The *Annales* began with the friendship of the historians Lucien Febvre (1878–1956) and Marc Bloch (1886–1944), who together founded the journal *Annales d'histoire économiques et sociales* in 1929. Bloch was killed as part of the Resistance in 1944. Lefebvre met both Bloch and Febvre in Strasbourg.

Aristocracy: a class whose historic wealth or legal privileges give it a superior social and political position. Lefebvre interpreted 1789 as a revolution against the very concept of aristocracy.

Aristocratic reaction: the theory that the aristocracy at the end of the eighteenth century were bitter at their exclusion from chief positions in the army, the church, the courts, and the provincial administration. As a result they both tried to push the bourgeoisie out from these posts, and increased the rent they exerted from their peasants under seigneurial rights (feudal privileges such as payments or labor services demanded by landowners from laborers who worked their estates). The theory was defended by the historians Philippe Sagnac and Georges Lefebvre, though later attacked.

August Decrees: a series of decrees issued on August 4, 1789, when the deputies of the National Assembly voted to abolish feudalism and renounce their titles and their ancient privileges. The vote was strongly influenced by their fear of peasant unrest, and was accompanied by a generous scheme of compensation.

Bastille: the royal fortress on the eastern edge of Paris, which acted as both a prison and an arsenal. It was overwhelmed by crowds of Parisians on July 14, 1789, an event commemorated today as a national holiday.

Bicentenary: a term used to describe the two-hundredth anniversary of an event.

Bourbon dynasty: the dynasty that ruled France from the accession of Henri IV in 1589 through to the deposition of Charles X in 1830. Louis XVI was a Bourbon.

Bourgeoisie: a word coined in medieval France to refer loosely to urban groups who made their wealth through trade or services rather than from ownership of land. The economist and political theorist Karl Marx used the term more specifically to designate the class of property owners who had taken power from the old aristocracy and made vast fortunes out of capitalism by exploiting the working classes.

Cahiers de doléances: registers of grievances collected from all three estates of France (the clergy, the nobility, and the common people) to act as a guide to deputies in the Estates General, a national assembly that met in May 1789.

Capitalism: an economic system based on private ownership, private enterprise, and the maximization of profit. Marxist scholars argue that the French Revolution facilitated the growth of capitalism through abolishing forms of hereditary property and scrapping economic regulation.

Class struggle: a key term within Marxist analysis, according to which historical change is driven by the conflict between different social groups fighting for control over the means of production.

Cold War (1947–91): a period of protracted tension between the United States and the Soviet Union between 1947 and the collapse of the Soviet Union in 1991. It was marked by an arms race, a number of proxy wars, and intense ideological rivalry.

Communism: an ideology that aims at the abolition of private property, an end to capitalism, and the creation of an egalitarian society.

Comparative history: an approach to history intended to establish meaningful comparisons between different historical entities or contexts.

Conservatism: an ideology that tends to see human nature as individualistic and acquisitive. It privileges the survival of established institutions and the maintenance of traditional authority and norms.

Consumerism: a social order and an ideology that encourages the ever-increasing acquisition of goods and services. Lefebvre believed that consumerism undermined the social hierarchies of the Old Regime.

Corporate bodies: within the absolutist monarchy, while only the king had sovereignty, he was expected to uphold the rights and privileges of particular organizations, such as the *parlements*, the guilds, and the academies.

Counterrevolution: a secondary revolution aimed at scaling back or reversing the results of a revolution.

Declaration of the Rights of Man: laws adopted by the Constituent Assembly on August 23, 1789, proclaimed as a series of rights and freedoms that were seen to be universal, belonging by nature to humans everywhere.

Deputy: an elected representative; deputies were elected from across France to sit in the Estates General at the start of 1789.

Direct democracy: a system in which, rather than express their sovereignty indirectly through electing representatives to speak for them, the people retain full sovereignty themselves. After the revolution, the activists known as the *sans-culottes* were firm believers in direct democracy as carried out in their neighborhood clubs.

Émigré: a term that refers to individuals who have left their home country, often for political reasons. During the French Revolution, many émigrés were aristocrats who left France to live elsewhere in Europe because they disagreed with the revolution or felt their lives and property were in danger.

Enlightenment: a movement of late seventeenth- and eighteenth-century Europe that emphasized the use of reason to increase knowledge and improve society. Lefebvre associated the values of the Enlightenment with the bourgeoisie.

Estates General: the largest representative assembly in France, made up of deputies elected from each of the three orders (clergy, nobility, commoners). It had not met since 1614. Louis XVI was forced to convoke it in May 1789 to try to gain sanction for much-needed tax reforms.

Fascism: a political movement of the far right, based around authoritarian government and mass mobilization, which often includes militarist and nationalist elements. It was at the height of its influence in interwar Europe. Lefebvre saw fascism as the ideological enemy of everything the French Revolution stood for.

Feudalism: an economic and social system associated with medieval Europe, based on the reciprocal relationships between landowners and tenants based on military protection and obligated, agricultural labor.

Freemason: a member of a number of societies that spread through Europe from the eighteenth century, with many Masonic Lodges being formed in towns and cities. Freemasons showed a marked interest in Enlightenment ideas of toleration, free inquiry, unorthodox Christianity and the brotherhood of man.

Freethinker: one tending to hold views critical of traditional attitudes about society and especially about the teachings of religion. The heritage of freethinking in France was strongly linked with the eighteenth-century Enlightenment.

French Resistance: the underground struggle against the Nazi occupation of France (1940–4); Lefebvre's brother Théodore was executed for his role in these activities.

French Revolution: the political upheaval that broke out in France in 1789 and endured for a decade, leading to a dramatic period of reform, the proclamation of the French Republic in 1792, and the revolutionary violence of the Terror, in which many thousands were killed in the name of ideological purity because of factionalism in the post-revolution political environment.

Glorious Revolution (1688): the name commonly given to the overthrow of English king James II by an alliance of Parliamentarians and the Dutch ruler, William of Orange, who subsequently became William III of Great Britain, ruling jointly with his wife, Mary II (daughter of James II). The reestablishment of the monarchy under William of Orange and Queen Mary was conditional on their accepting the authority of Parliament in making law and marked a major evolution in English constitutional development.

Great Fear: swept through parts of the French countryside in the spring and summer of 1789. Paranoid rumors were spread about brigands on the roads, a deliberate attempt by the aristocrats to starve the peasants, and a plot orchestrated by the nobility to reverse the gains promised by the Estates General. The fear encouraged peasants to attack aristocratic property and to refuse to pay their taxes or manorial dues (feudal obligations owed to the local landlord).

History from below: sometimes attributed to Georges Lefebvre or Lucien Febvre, this historical school of thought tends to view history from the perspective not just of the rulers but also of the ruled.

Jacobin: also known as the Society of the Friends of the Constitution, the Jacobins were members of a political club that emerged during the French Revolution which provided the support-base for radical deputies. Jacobins demonstrated greater flexibility in their principles, willing to do anything to help save the Republic.

Left–wing politics: ideologically close to socialism, left-wing politics are variously linked to values like community, equality, and redistribution. The terms "right" and "left" were invented during the French Revolution.

Manorial system: a system under which a peasant or farmer owed manorial dues and impositions (feudal obligations) to the local landlord, which were paid either in labor or in coin.

Marxism: the political philosophy, social theory, and analytical approach derived from the writings and methods of the German philosopher and political theorist Karl Marx (1818–83). According to classical Marxist political theory, capitalism will be destroyed by its own contradictions and replaced with a more egalitarian communist system.

Materialism: the philosophical view that all facts (including facts about the course of human history) depend upon physical processes. According to Marxist analysis, "materialism" is the belief that history is driven by class struggle.

Monarchy: a system of government in which society is ruled by one person, a monarch, usually chosen by hereditary succession. France at the time of the revolution was ruled by monarchs from the Bourbon dynasty.

National Assembly: on June 17, 1789, the deputies of the Third Estate in the Estates General (that is, the people outside the aristocracy and the clergy) unanimously declared themselves to be the National Assembly and to represent the entirety of France. Sympathizers among some of the other orders defected to join them, and Louis XVI reluctantly accepted the creation of this new body, sometimes also called the Constituent Assembly. New elections in 1791 and 1792 saw the National Assembly replaced by the Legislative Assembly and the Convention.

National Guard: a group that emerged in July 1789 out of militias set up across France to protect law and order during the revolutionary crisis. Membership of the National Guard was at first restricted only to wealthier citizens, and was presented as a civic honor.

Nazi Party: an extreme right-wing political party that ruled Germany between 1933 and 1945, led by Adolf Hitler.

October Days: a period that saw crowds from Paris—especially market women—march to Versailles along with members of the National Guard on October 5 and 6, 1789. After demanding bread from the king, they then forced the royal family to come back to the city with them under escort.

Old Regime (*Ancien Régime*): the monarchical society that preceded 1789. It is a vague term, invented by the revolutionaries, to mark out their distance from the old order of things.

***Parlements*:** the numerous *parlements* under the old regime were bodies of magistrates who deliberated on royal edicts and voted taxes for the crown; from the reign of the Louis XV onwards, the relationship between the monarchy and *parlements* soured considerably.

Popular Front: the government of Léon Blum, France's first socialist prime minister, in 1936 and 1938, which represented a coalition of radicals, socialists and communists, healing the divisions on the left. It saw the passage of important welfare legislation.

Popular sovereignty: the idea that the people are and should be the source of all political authority in a state; it was a chief principle asserted in France in 1789.

Proletariat: the term used by Marx to denote the industrial working classes, who were exploited by capitalism and had nothing to lose from revolution; Marx believed that the proletariat would lead a future communist revolution.

Protestants: Christians who do not accept the authority of the Catholic Church in Rome but, rather, emphasize the importance of scriptural authority and the conscience of the individual believer over the place of the clergy and the sacraments. Ever since the sixteenth-century Reformation, when the first Protestants broke away from the authority of Rome, there has been a huge proliferation of different Protestant churches.

Republicanism: a wide-ranging political movement, defined primarily by its opposition to rule by a king or queen, and hence by extension often hostile to privilege and forms of social, legal and confessional inequality.

Revisionism: any movement in historiography (the writing of history) that calls formerly accepted narratives into question; in the case of the French Revolution, this occurred in two phases, with the "soft revisionism" of Cobban in the 1960s and the "hard revisionism" of Furet in the 1970s. In the field of the French Revolution, revisionist historians are united only by their skepticism towards the traditional Marxist theory of a bourgeois revolution.

Revolutionary Tribunal: created by the Convention in 1793 as a special court to speedily sentence and execute enemies of the revolution.

Right-wing politics: ideologically conservative and linked to principles such as individualism, traditional values, and an opposition to government interference. The terms "right and "left" were invented during the French Revolution.

Sans-culottes: urban radicals, largely recruited from the ranks of artisans, who were strongly in favor of popular democracy and social equality. They dominated Paris politics from 1792 to 1794.

Social history: a form of historical research that examines the structures of society such as class divisions and the family unit as well as the experiences and outlooks of men and women from all strata of society, as opposed to just the political elite.

Social sciences: academic disciplines including psychology, economics, sociology, social anthropology, and political science, that seek to use scientific techniques to understand the functioning of societies.

Socialism: a political movement that the British historian Eric Hobsbawm believed to have been defined in the early nineteenth century; socialists seek to reform capitalism in order to create a more just and equal society. Marxism is one variant of socialism among many.

Sorbonne: a university in Paris. In 1885 a chair in French revolutionary history was created at the Sorbonne for the historian Alphonse Aulard, and it was occupied by many distinguished French historians including Philippe Sagnac, Georges Lefebvre, Albert Soboul, and Michel Vovelle.

Soviet Union (1922–91): a communist state based upon principles of Marxist-Leninism (trying to implement communism using a dictatorship). It encompassed Russia and surrounding states in Eastern Europe and central Asia.

The Terror: occurred during the years 1792–4 and emerged in parallel to the establishment of the French Republic. It involved the suspension of civil liberties, the defense of the country in times of war, and the ruthless elimination of presumed enemies.

Third Estate: in French society there were three "estates" or orders: the clergy (first estate), the nobility (second estate) and the commons (third estate). The third estate made up the vast majority of the French population. In June 1789 the deputies representing the Third Estate in the Estates General rebelled against the existing framework and declared themselves the National Assembly.

Third Republic: France's longest-lasting constitutional settlement, in place from 1870 down to the occupation of France in 1940. It was committed to values inherited from the revolution—such as equality before the law, freedom of expression and the separation of Church and state. Anti-republican forces had no single ideology, but were determined to overthrow a system they viewed as compromised, corrupt, and ineffectual.

Valmy, Jemappes, Fleurus: key victories won by the citizen armies of the French Republic in 1792, 1793 and 1794 respectively, not only saving France from foreign invasion but also pushing the Austrian armies back into the Low Countries. These were highly symbolic victories because they were won by the "nation in arms."

Venality: rife in eighteenth-century France, this refers to the royal policy of selling offices related to the administration of the kingdom (such as tax collecting) in order to raise funds.

Versailles: located just outside of Paris, this was the palace of the French kings. It was extended and embellished under the reign of Louis XIV. In the October Days in 1789, the Parisian population forced the royal family to return to the capital.

Vichy France: a short-lived French government, imposed following France's defeat at the hands of Nazi Germany in May 1940. France was divided between a northern zone placed under direct German occupation, and a southern zone ruled by the collaborationist Vichy government.

World War I (1914–18): a conflict between the Central Powers (Germany, Austria-Hungary, the Ottoman Empire) and the Entente (Britain, France, Russia, Japan) that was waged in Europe, the European colonies, and Asia.

World War II (1939–45): the global conflict that pitted the Axis powers of Nazi Germany, Fascist Italy, and Imperial Japan against the Allied nations of Britain, the United States, and the Soviet Union. The war ended following the Allied invasion of Germany in 1945.

PEOPLE MENTIONED IN THE TEXT

Alphonse Aulard (1849–1928) was a French scholar, who dominated revolutionary historiography through his chair at the Sorbonne after 1885, and his publication of vital primary sources and official documents.

Jacques Bainville (1879–1936) was a follower of royalist Charles Maurras and *Action Française* who wrote several highly counterrevolutionary histories of France.

Keith Michael Baker (b. 1938) is professor of intellectual history at Stanford University in the US and one of the most important collaborators with François Furet in studying the political languages of eighteenth-century France. See his important essay collection *Inventing the French Revolution* (1990).

Abbé Augustin (de) Barruel (1741–1820) was a London-based writer who first suggested that the revolution had been the work of a cabal of Protestants, Freemasons and atheist philosophers.

C. B. A. (Betty) Behrens (1904–89) was a historian of eighteenth-century European societies who gave an early rebuttal of Marxist interpretations.

Marc Bloch (1886–1944) was one of the founders of the *Annales* school in historiography, celebrated for his work on the royal touch and the medieval economy. The Nazis executed him for his role in the Resistance.

Léon Blum (1872–1950) was France's first socialist prime minister; he oversaw the two turbulent Popular Front governments in 1936 and 1938, predicated on an alliance of left-wing parties.

Crane Brinton (1898–1968) was a Harvard-based historian of revolutionary movements. In his classic book *Anatomy of Revolution* (1938) he compared the progress of the revolution to the development of a dangerous fever.

Charles-Alexandre de Calonne (1734–1802) was a minister under Louis XVI. He formulated an ambitious reform program in 1786–7, which was rejected by the Assembly of Notables in 1787. He fled the country into exile in 1789.

Richard Cobb (1917–96) was a historian at Oxford University, renowned for his interest in the forgotten, ordinary men and women caught up in the French Revolution.

Alfred Cobban (1901–68) was a British historian of France based at the University of London. Cobban began the wave of revisionism that questioned the accuracy of the Marxist understanding of 1789.

Marvin Cox is a professor at the University of Connecticut who specializes in revolutionary historiography.

William Doyle (b. 1942) is professor of history at the University of Bristol and leading revisionist interpreter of the French Revolution. He has published classic survey works and recent studies on the European aristocracy.

Jean Egret was a French historian who taught at Poitiers University and specialized in the study of public opinion and political factionalism in the years leading up to 1789. He described the period 1787–9 as the "pre-revolution."

Lucien Febvre (1878–1956) was one of the founders of the *Annales* school in historiography; he produced important studies of early modern geography, religious culture, and the history of the book.

Robert Forster is professor of history at Johns Hopkins University, famed for his work on Toulouse and the eighteenth-century nobility.

François Furet (1927–97) was a Marxist who, disillusioned with Soviet communism, abandoned social explanations in the 1970s to become the most important French historian of the revolution through his emphasis on politics, culture, and discourse.

Pierre Gaxotte (1895–1982) was a follower of Charles Maurras, and a counterrevolutionary scholar who wrote a history of the revolution in 1928 and a general survey of Louis XV's France in 1933.

Jacques Godechot (1907–89) was a French historian influenced by Marxism and the *Annales* who, along with Palmer, was a pioneer of Atlantic history.

François Guizot (1787–1874) was a historian and liberal statesman in the 1830s and 1840s who frequently wrote on the connection between modern and medieval France.

Jürgen Habermas (b. 1929) is a German sociologist, celebrated for his work on communicative reason and the development of a "public sphere." His account of how the public sphere emerged in the eighteenth century has been a huge influence on a variety of political and cultural historians, including Keith Baker and T. C. W. Blanning.

Norman Hampson (1922–2011) was a British historian of France based at York University who wrote important works on the Enlightenment, the social history of the French Revolution and Robespierre.

Carla Hesse (b. 1956) is a professor in French history at the University of California, Berkeley. She has published important works on the print trade, women in the Enlightenment, and the legal culture of the Terror.

Adolf Hitler (1889–1945) was leader of the Nazi Party and dictator of Germany between 1933 and 1945. His expansionist policies provoked World War II.

Eric Hobsbawm (1917–2012) was a British Marxist historian who spent the bulk of his career at Birkbeck University, and who wrote widely and penetratingly on aspects of nineteenth- and twentieth-century European history.

Lynn Hunt (b. 1945) is professor of history at the University of Los Angeles and is the most influential cultural historian of the French Revolution. She has written widely on political culture, gender, and global history, and has been influential in promoting the "cultural turn"—a school of thought that swept across the humanities in the 1980s and 1990s. Under the influence of French philosophical ideas, it launched an attack on grand narratives in order to pay more attention to questions of meaning, representation, and subjectivity.

Jean Jaurès (1859–1914) was the leader of the French Socialist Party from 1902 until 1914; a profound anti-militarist, Jaurès stood for a highly moralized and idealistic vision of French socialism, in contrast to more materialist and determinist Marxist thought.

Colin Jones (b. 1947) is professor of history at Queen Mary University of London and a leading expert on eighteenth-century France and the history of medicine.

Ernest Labrousse (1895–1988) was a socialist and close ally of Marc Bloch, and a pioneer in statistical and serial economic history. He is famous for his work on price fluctuations.

Gwynne Lewis (1933–2014) was a professor at the University of Warwick, who wrote on artisan politics in France and Britain and the counterrevolution.

Abraham Lincoln (1809–65) was the president of the United States whose commitment to the abolition of slavery precipitated the American Civil War, in which he led the North to victory.

Louis XVI (1754–93) was the king of France from 1774 to 1792. He was initially hugely popular with the French nation. His decision to help the American colonists brought a diplomatic victory but grave financial problems, and the attempt to reform government structures created the French Revolution in 1789. Ill-suited to becoming a constitutional monarch, as was envisaged in 1789, Louis made an abortive attempt to flee the country in 1791 and was overthrown on August 10, 1792. He was executed as a traitor in January 1793.

Marie-Antoinette (1755–93) was an Austrian princess who, through marriage to Louis XVI, became queen of France in 1774. Linked to numerous scandals, she was a deeply unpopular figure, and was guillotined in November 1793.

John Markoff (b. 1942) is professor of sociology at the University of Pittsburgh, and has studied the actions of the French peasantry during the 1790s as part of his wider interest in the history of democratization.

Karl Marx (1818–83) was a German economist, historian, philosopher, and social theorist whose historical materialist conception of history and economic writings provided the ideological basis for communism.

Albert Mathiez (1874–1932) was born in the same year as Lefebvre and preceded him as chief of the Société des Études Robespierristes, which he founded. Mathiez had specialized in the history of the church, before Lefebvre's early writings awakened him to economic history, as represented by *La Vie chère et le mouvement social sous la Terreur* (1927). Unlike Lefebvre, he was a committed communist.

Sarah Maza (b. 1953) is professor of history at Northwestern University and has published widely on legal culture in France from the eighteenth to the twentieth century.

Jules Michelet (1798–1874) was the foremost French historian of the nineteenth century, whose ecstatic *Histoire de la Révolution française* appeared between 1847 and 1853. His emphasis on the historian's empathy with the unknown and ordinary individuals in history exerted an enormous influence.

François-Auguste Mignet (1796–1884) was a historian who wrote an important early history of the French Revolution in 1824. Mignet already saw the revolution as a clash of two different classes of people, although these classes were defined partly in historic and ethnic, rather than economic, terms.

Honoré-Gabriel Riqueti de Mirabeau (1749–91) was a powerful and popular orator, but Lefebvre insisted that he was not in control of events in 1789. He had absented himself from the vote on August 4 and passionately defended the king's right to an absolute veto.

Napoleon Bonaparte (1769–1821) was born in Corsica and rose spectacularly through the French army to become general; in 1799 he overthrew the French republic in a coup d'état, and in 1804 declared himself emperor. His military and political genius made him master of Europe until his defeat at Waterloo in 1815.

Robert Roswell (R. R.) Palmer (1909–2002) was an American historian based at Princeton whose most famous work was the two-volume *Age of Democratic Revolution* (1959–64).

Jean Renoir (1894–1979) was a prolific and brilliant French filmmaker, actor and author; his films from the late 1930s, such as *La Grande Illusion*, were powerfully shaped by his leftist and anti-militarist politics.

Maximilien Robespierre (1758–94) was a key orator in the Jacobin club and dominated the Committee of Public Safety that ruled France as a revolutionary dictatorship between 1793 and 1794 and implemented the Terror. After turning on many of his former allies, Robespierre himself was overthrown by members of the Convention in 1794 and guillotined.

George Rudé (1910–93) was a British Marxist historian who did pioneering work on the role on crowds and politics in the French Revolution and in Britain in the age of reform.

Philippe Sagnac (1868–1954) was a French historian who preceded Lefebvre in the chair of revolutionary history at the Sorbonne and encouraged research into the peasantry. Sagnac advanced the thesis of an "aristocratic reaction."

Simon Schama (b. 1945) is a cultural historian at the University of Columbia who has written on a range of topics, from seventeenth-century Holland to eighteenth-century France and wide-ranging histories of Britain and the Jewish people.

James Scott (b. 1936) is an anthropologist and political scientist who has written extensively on peasant movements in Asia and the functions of the state. His classic work, "Weapons of the Weak," has investigated the scope for popular resistance against authority.

William Sewell, Jr. (b. 1940) is a professor at the University of Chicago and a leading historian of eighteenth- and nineteenth-century French social and cultural history. He has also written on historical method, calling for closer relations between historians and social scientists.

Abbé Sieyès (1748–1836) was the author of the classic pamphlet *Qu'est-ce que le Tiers État?* A prime mover in creating the National Assembly, his opposition to the abolition of manorial dues and the nationalization of church land meant that by the end of 1789, in the view of Lefebvre, he had "ceased to be a source of inspiration to the Third Estate."

Theda Skocpol (b. 1947) is professor of sociology at Harvard, renowned for her comparative work on revolutions and state-formation. Like Lefebvre, she put emphasis on the importance of agrarian issues in provoking rebellion.

Albert Soboul (1914–82) was one of Georges Lefebvre's students and the most important defender of the Marxist interpretation of the French Revolution. He is remembered for his brilliant 1958 work on the popular movement and the sans-culottes.

Timothy Tackett (b. 1945) is a professor at the University of California who has written important works on the National Assembly, the crisis of 1791 when the king tried to flee France, and religious opposition in rural France.

Hippolyte Taine (1828–93) was a philosopher and critic who wrote the most damning account of the French Revolution, inflected by his experiences in the Paris Commune; he depicted the sentimental abstractions of the revolution leading to terrible atrocities, in which the common people behaved like savage beasts.

George V. Taylor (1919–2011) was an American historian based at Chapel Hill, in North Carolina, who wrote a series of landmark articles on the French eighteenth-century economy in the 1960s.

E. P. Thompson (1924–1993) was the foremost British social historian of the latter half of the twentieth century; a passionate Marxist, Thompson was author of the seminal *The Making of the English Working Class* (1963). Unlike Hobsbawm he left the Communist Party after the Hungarian uprising.

Charles Tilly (1929–2008) was a political scientist based at the University of Michigan who produced pioneering works on historical sociology, investigating in particular popular rebellion and resistance.

Alexis de Tocqueville (1805–59) was a statesman, philosopher, traveler and historian. He made his name through his study of American democracy, and in 1856 wrote *L'Ancien Régime et la Révolution*, showing how the Jacobins simply took over and completed the centralizing efforts of the French monarchy.

Michel Vovelle (b. 1933) is a distinguished professor and historian of the French Revolution, who has occupied the chair at the Sorbonne in the history of the French Revolution since 1982. He has attempted to reconcile Marxist and *Annales* approaches, and has worked extensively on the history of mentalities.

Max Weber (1864–1920) was a German founder of sociology, who gave an account of the historical genesis of bourgeois attitudes in *The Protestant Ethic and the Spirit of Capitalism* from 1904.

WORKS CITED

WORKS CITED

Aston, Nigel. *Religion and Revolution in France, 1780–1804*. Basingstoke: Macmillan, 2000.

Aulard, Alphonse. *Histoire politique de la Révolution française: Origines et de développement de la démocratie française 1789–1804*. Paris, 1901.

Bainville, Jacques. *Histoire de France*. Paris: Fayard, 1924.

Baker, Keith Michael. *Inventing the French Revolution: Essays on French Political Culture in the Eighteenth Century*. Cambridge: Cambridge University Press, 1990.

Barruel, Abbé Augustin. *Mémoires pour server à l'histoire du Jacobinisme*. Paris, 1797–8.

Behrens, C. B. A. "Nobles, Privileges and Taxes in France at the End of the Ancien Regime." *Economic History Review* 15 (1962–3): 451–75.

Beik, Paul. Preface to Georges Lefebvre, *The French Revolution: From its Origins to 1793*. New York: Columbia University Press, 1962, ix–xv.

Blanc, Louis. *Histoire de la Révolution française*, 12 vols. Paris,1847–62.

Blanning, T. C. W. *The French Revolution in Germany: Occupation and Resistance in the Rhineland, 1792–1802*. Oxford: Clarendon Press, 1983.

Brinton, Crane. *The Anatomy of Revolution*. New York: Norton, 1938.

Buzzi, Stéphane, "Georges Lefebvre (1874–1959), ou une histoire sociale possible." *Le Mouvement Social*, no. 200 (2002–2003): 177–95.

Chaussinand-Nogaret, Guy. *La Noblesse au XVIIIe siècle. De la féodalité aux lumières*. Paris: Hachette, 1976.

Cobb, Richard. "Georges Lefebvre." In *A Second Identity: Essays on France and French History*, 84–110. Oxford: Oxford University Press, 1969.

Les Armées révolutionnaires: Instrument de la Terreur dans les départements, avril 1793–floréal an II. 2 vols. Paris: Mouton, 1961–3.

Cobban, Alfred. *Aspects of the French Revolution*. London: Jonathan Cape, 1968.

"The Myth of the French Revolution". Inaugural lecture, University College, London, May 6,1954. Arden Library, 1978.

The Social Interpretation of the French Revolution. Cambridge: Cambridge University Press, 1964.

Cox, Marvin. "Furet, Cobban, Marx: The Revision of the 'Orthodoxy' Revisited." *Historical Reflections* 27, no. 1 (2001): 49–77.

Crossley, Ceri. *French Historians and Romanticism: Thierry, Guizot, the Saint-Simonians, Quinet, Michelet.* New York and London: Routledge, 2002.

Daudet, Léon. *Deux idoles sanguinaires: La Révolution et son fils Bonaparte.* Paris: Albin Michel, 1939.

Desan, Suzanne. *The Family on Trial in Revolutionary France.* Berkeley: University of California Press, 2004.

Doyle, William. *Aristocracy and Its Enemies in the Age of Revolution.* Oxford: Oxford University Press, 2009.

Origins of the French Revolution. Oxford: Oxford University Press, 1980.

Dubois, Laurent. *A Colony of Citizens: Revolution and Slave Emancipation in the French Caribbean, 1787–1804.* Chapel Hill, NC: University of North Carolina Press, 2004.

Edelmann, Dan. *The Enlightenment: A Genealogy.* Chicago, IL: University of Chicago Press, 2010.

Egret, Jean, *La Prévolution française.* Paris: Presses Universitaires de France, 1962.

Forster, Robert. *The Nobility of Toulouse in the Eighteenth Century: A Social and Economic Study.* Baltimore, MD: Johns Hopkins University Press, 1960.

Furet, François. "The French Revolution Is Over." Translated by E. Forster. In *Interpreting the French Revolution*, 1–80. Cambridge: Cambridge University Press, 1981.

La Révolution: De Turgot à Jules Ferry, 1770–1880. Paris: Hachette, 1988.

"Sur le catéchisme de la Révolution française." *Annales: économies, sociétés, civilisations* 26, no. 2 (1971): 269–77.

Gaxotte, Pierre. *La Révolution française.* Paris: Fayard,1928.

Godechot, Jacques. *France and the Atlantic Revolution of the Eighteenth Century.* New York: The Free Press, 1965.

"The Social Interpretation of the French Revolution." *Revue Historique* 235 (1966): 205–9.

Un Jury pour la Révolution. Paris: Robert Laffont, 1974.

Goldstone, Jack A. "The Social Origins of the French Revolution Revisited." In *From Deficit to Deluge: The Origins of the French Revolution*, edited by Dale Van Kley and Thomas E. Kaiser, 67–103. Stanford, CA: Stanford University Press, 2011.

Habermas, Jürgen. *The Structural Transformation of the Public Sphere: An Inquiry into a Category of Bourgeois Society*. Translated by Thomas Berger. Cambridge: Polity Press, 1989.

Hampson, Norman. "The French Revolution and Its Historians." In *The Permanent Revolution*, edited by Geoffrey Best, 211–34. London: Fontana, 1988.

Hesse, Carla. "The New Jacobins." *French Historical Studies* 32, no. 4 (2009): 663–70.

Higonnet, Patrice. *Goodness Beyond Virtue: Jacobins during the French Revolution*. Cambridge, MA: Harvard University Press, 1998.

Hobsbawm, Eric. *Primitive Rebels: Studies in Archaic Forms of Social Movement in the Nineteenth and Twentieth Centuries*. Manchester: Manchester University Press, 1959.

Hufton, Olwen. *Women and the Limits of Citizenship in the French Revolution*. Toronto: University of Toronto Press, 1992.

Hunt, Lynn. *Politics, Culture and Class in the French Revolution*. Berkeley, CA: University of California Press, 1984.

Hunt, Lynn, and Victoria Bonnell, eds. *Beyond the Cultural Turn: New Directions in the Study of Society and Culture*. Berkeley, CA: University of California Press, 1999.

Hunt, Lynn, Suzanne Desan, and William Nelson, eds. *The French Revolution in Global Perspective*. Ithaca, NY: Cornell University Press, 2013.

Hutton, Sir Patrick. *History as an Art of Memory.* Hanover: University of Vermont, 1993.

Hyslop, Beatrice. "Georges Lefebvre, Historian." *French Historical Studies* 1 (1960): 265–82.

Jaurès, Jean. *Histoire socialiste de la Révolution française*. Edited by A. Mathiez. 8 vols. Paris: Libre de l'Humanité, 1922–4.

Jones, Colin. "Bourgeois Revolution Revivified: 1789 and Social Change." In *Rewriting the French Revolution*, edited by Colin Lucas, 69–118. Oxford: Oxford University Press, 1991.

The Charitable Imperative: Hospitals and Nursing in Ancien Regime and Revolutionary France. London: Routledge, 1989.

Jones, Peter M. "Georges Lefebvre and the Peasant Revolution: Fifty Years On." *French Historical Studies* 16 (1990): 545–63.

The Peasantry in the French Revolution. Cambridge: Cambridge University Press, 1988.

Kaplan, Stephen J. *Farewell Revolution: Disputed Legacies—France 1789/1989*. Ithaca, NY: Cornell University Press, 1995.

Kley, Dale Van, and Thomas Kaiser, eds. *From Deficit to Deluge: The Origins of the French Revolution*. Stanford, CA: Stanford University Press, 2011.

Kwass, Michael. *Privilege and the Politics of Taxation in Eighteenth-Century France: Liberté, Égalité, Fiscalité.* Cambridge: Cambridge University Press, 2000.

Lefebvre, Georges. "Avenir de l'histoire." In Études sur la Révolution française, 269–87. Paris: Presses Universitaires de France, 1954.

The Coming of the French Revolution. Translated by Robert R. Palmer. Princeton, NJ: Princeton University Press, 2005.

Le Directoire. Paris: Armand Colin, 1946.

Études orléanaises: Contribution à l'étude des structures sociales à la fin du XVIIIe siècle. 2 vols. Paris: Commission d'histoire économique et sociale de la Révolution française, 1962–3.

Études sur la Révolution française. Paris: Presses Universitaires de France, 1954.

"Les Foules révolutionnaires." In *La Foule: Quatrième semaine internationale de synthèse*, edited by Paul Alphandéry, Georges Bon, Georges Hardy, Georges Lefebvre, and Eugène Dupréel. Paris: Felix Alcan, 1934.

La Grande Peur de 1789. Paris: A. Colin, 1932.

"Les Mouvements des prix et les origines de la Révolution française." *Annales historiques de la Révolution française* 9 (1937): 288–329.

Quatre-Vingt Neuf. 1939.

"The Myth of the French Revolution." *Annales historiques de la Révolution française* 28 (1956): 337–45.

Napoléon. Paris: P. Alcan, 1935. *Questions agraires au temps de la Terreur*. Strasbourg: Fenig, 1932.

La Révolution française. Paris: Presses Universitaires de France, 1951.

Lewis, Gwynne. *The French Revolution: Rethinking the Debate*. London: Routledge, 1993.

Markoff, John. *The Abolition of Feudalism: Peasants, Lords and Legislators in the French Revolution*. University Park, PA: Pennsylvania State University Press, 1996.

"Violence, Emancipation, and Democracy: The Countryside and the French Revolution." *American Historical Review* 100 (1995): 360–85.

Karl Marx, *Contribution to the Critique of Hegel's Philosophy of Right*. 1843.

On the Jewish Question. 1843–4.

Mathiez, Abert. *The French* Revolution [1922–7]. Translated by C. A. Phillips. New York: Russell and Russell, 1962.

La Vie chère et le mouvement social sous la Terreur. Paris: Fayard, 1927.

Maza, Sarah. *The Myth of the French Bourgeoisie: An Essay in the Social Imaginary, 1750–1850*. Cambridge, MA: Harvard University Press, 2003.

Private Lives and Public Affairs: The Causes Celebres of Prerevolutionary France. Berkeley, CA, and London: University of California Press, 1993.

Mazauric, Claude. "Les Chaussées sont désertes, plus de passants sur les chemins: La SER dans la tourmente: 1940–1945." *Annales historiques de la Révolution française* 353 (2008): 169–207.

McPhee, Peter. *Living the French Revolution, 1789–99*. Basingstoke: Palgrave Macmillan, 2009.

Michelet, Jules. *Histoire de la Révolution française*. 7 vols. Paris, 1847–53.

Ory, Pascal. *Une Nation pour la mémoire: 1889, 1939, 1989, trois jubilés révolutionnaires*. Paris: Presses de la Fondation nationale des sciences politiques, 1992.

Palmer, Robert R. *The Age of Democratic Revolutions: A Political History of Europe and America 1760–1800*. 2 vols. Princeton, NJ: Princeton University Press, 1964.

Price, Munro. *The Fall of the French Monarchy: Louis XVI, Marie Antoinette and the Baron de Breteuil*. London: Palgrave Macmillan, 2002.

Reddy, William. *Money and Liberty in Western Europe: A Critique of Historical Understanding*. Cambridge: Cambridge University Press, 1987.

Root, Hilton. "The Case against Georges Lefebvre's Peasant Revolution." *History Workshop Journal* 28 (1989): 88–102.

Rudé, George. *The Crowd in the French Revolution*. Oxford: Oxford University Press, 1959.

Schama, Simon. *Citizens: A Chronicle of the French Revolution*. London: Penguin, 1989.

Scott, Joan. *Only Paradoxes to Offer: French Feminists and the Rights of Man*. Cambridge, MA: Harvard University Press, 1996.

Scott, John C. *Weapons of the Weak: Everyday Forms of Peasant Resistance*. New Haven, CT, and London: Yale University Press, 1985.

Sewell, Jr., William H. *A Rhetoric of Bourgeois Revolution: The Abbé Sièyes and What Is the Third Estate?* Durham, NC: Duke University Press, 1994.

Shovlin, John. *The Political Economy of Virtue: Luxury, Patriotism and the Origins of the French Revolution*. Ithaca, NY: Cornell University Press, 2006.

Sieyès, Abbé Emanuel Joseph. *Qu'est-ce que le Tiers État?* (What is the Third Estate?) January 1789.

Skocpol, Theda. *States and Social Revolutions: A Comparative Analysis of France, Russia and China*. Cambridge: Cambridge University Press, 1979.

Soboul, Albert. "Classes and Class Struggles during the French Revolution." *Science and Society* 17 (1953): 238–57.

Les Sans-culottes parisiens en l'an II: Mouvement populaire et gouvernement révolutionnaire, 2 juin 1793–9 thermidor an II. Paris: Clavreuil, 1958.

Sonenscher, Michael. *Before the Deluge: Public Debt, Inequality and the Intellectual Origins of the French Revolution*. Princeton, NJ: Princeton University Press, 2007.

Work and Wages: Natural Law, Politics, and Eighteenth-Century France. Cambridge: Cambridge University Press, 1989.

Spang, Rebecca. "Paradigms and Paranoia: How Modern is the French Revolution?" *American Historical Review* 108, no. 1 (2003): 119–47.

Stone, Bailey. *Reinterpreting the French Revolution: A Global-Historical Perspective*. Cambridge: Cambridge University Press, 2002.

Tackett, Timothy. "Collective Panics in the Early French Revolution, 1789–1791: A Comparative Perspective." *French History* 17 (2003): 149–71.

"Introduction." In Georges Lefebvre, *The Coming of the French Revolution*, vii–xxx. Princeton, NJ: Princeton University Press, 2005.

"Nobles and Third Estate in the Revolutionary Dynamic of the National Assembly, 1789–90." *American Historical Review* 94 (1989): 271–301.

Taine, Hippolyte. *Les Origines de la France contemporaine*. 5 vols. Paris, 1875–93.

Taylor, George V. "Noncapitalist Wealth and the Origins of the French Revolution." *American Historical Review* 72 (1967): 469–96.

"Types of Capitalism in Eighteenth-Century France." *English Historical Review* 79 (1964): 478–97.

Thompson, E. P. *The Making of the English Working Class*. London: Victor Gollancz, 1963.

Tilly, Charles. *The Vendée*. Cambridge, MA: Harvard University Press, 1964.

Tocqueville, Alexis de. *L'Ancien Régime et la Révolution. Paris, 1856.*

Vovelle, Michel. *La Mentalité révolutionnaire: Société et mentalités sous la Révolution française* (1789–1989). Paris: Éditions Sociales, 1985.

Weber, Max. *The Protestant Ethic and the Spirit of Capitalism.* 1905

Wilson, Stephen. "A View of the Past: Action Française Historiography and its Socio-political Function." *Historical Journal* 19 (1976): 135–61.

Woloch, Isser. *The New Regime: Transformations of the French Civic Order, 1789–1920s*. New York: Norton, 1995.

THE MACAT LIBRARY
BY DISCIPLINE

AFRICANA STUDIES

Chinua Achebe's *An Image of Africa: Racism in Conrad's Heart of Darkness*
W. E. B. Du Bois's *The Souls of Black Folk*
Zora Neale Huston's *Characteristics of Negro Expression*
Martin Luther King Jr's *Why We Can't Wait*
Toni Morrison's *Playing in the Dark: Whiteness in the American Literary Imagination*

ANTHROPOLOGY

Arjun Appadurai's *Modernity at Large: Cultural Dimensions of Globalisation*
Philippe Ariès's *Centuries of Childhood*
Franz Boas's *Race, Language and Culture*
Kim Chan & Renée Mauborgne's *Blue Ocean Strategy*
Jared Diamond's *Guns, Germs & Steel: the Fate of Human Societies*
Jared Diamond's *Collapse: How Societies Choose to Fail or Survive*
E. E. Evans-Pritchard's *Witchcraft, Oracles and Magic Among the Azande*
James Ferguson's *The Anti-Politics Machine*
Clifford Geertz's *The Interpretation of Cultures*
David Graeber's *Debt: the First 5000 Years*
Karen Ho's *Liquidated: An Ethnography of Wall Street*
Geert Hofstede's *Culture's Consequences: Comparing Values, Behaviors, Institutes and Organizations across Nations*
Claude Lévi-Strauss's *Structural Anthropology*
Jay Macleod's *Ain't No Makin' It: Aspirations and Attainment in a Low-Income Neighborhood*
Saba Mahmood's *The Politics of Piety: The Islamic Revival and the Feminist Subject*
Marcel Mauss's *The Gift*

BUSINESS

Jean Lave & Etienne Wenger's *Situated Learning*
Theodore Levitt's *Marketing Myopia*
Burton G. Malkiel's *A Random Walk Down Wall Street*
Douglas McGregor's *The Human Side of Enterprise*
Michael Porter's *Competitive Strategy: Creating and Sustaining Superior Performance*
John Kotter's *Leading Change*
C. K. Prahalad & Gary Hamel's *The Core Competence of the Corporation*

CRIMINOLOGY

Michelle Alexander's *The New Jim Crow: Mass Incarceration in the Age of Colorblindness*
Michael R. Gottfredson & Travis Hirschi's *A General Theory of Crime*
Richard Herrnstein & Charles A. Murray's *The Bell Curve: Intelligence and Class Structure in American Life*
Elizabeth Loftus's *Eyewitness Testimony*
Jay Macleod's *Ain't No Makin' It: Aspirations and Attainment in a Low-Income Neighborhood*
Philip Zimbardo's *The Lucifer Effect*

ECONOMICS

Janet Abu-Lughod's *Before European Hegemony*
Ha-Joon Chang's *Kicking Away the Ladder*
David Brion Davis's *The Problem of Slavery in the Age of Revolution*
Milton Friedman's *The Role of Monetary Policy*
Milton Friedman's *Capitalism and Freedom*
David Graeber's *Debt: the First 5000 Years*
Friedrich Hayek's *The Road to Serfdom*
Karen Ho's *Liquidated: An Ethnography of Wall Street*

John Maynard Keynes's *The General Theory of Employment, Interest and Money*
Charles P. Kindleberger's *Manias, Panics and Crashes*
Robert Lucas's *Why Doesn't Capital Flow from Rich to Poor Countries?*
Burton G. Malkiel's *A Random Walk Down Wall Street*
Thomas Robert Malthus's *An Essay on the Principle of Population*
Karl Marx's *Capital*
Thomas Piketty's *Capital in the Twenty-First Century*
Amartya Sen's *Development as Freedom*
Adam Smith's *The Wealth of Nations*
Nassim Nicholas Taleb's *The Black Swan: The Impact of the Highly Improbable*
Amos Tversky's & Daniel Kahneman's *Judgment under Uncertainty: Heuristics and Biases*
Mahbub Ul Haq's *Reflections on Human Development*
Max Weber's *The Protestant Ethic and the Spirit of Capitalism*

FEMINISM AND GENDER STUDIES

Judith Butler's *Gender Trouble*
Simone De Beauvoir's *The Second Sex*
Michel Foucault's *History of Sexuality*
Betty Friedan's *The Feminine Mystique*
Saba Mahmood's *The Politics of Piety: The Islamic Revival and the Feminist Subject*
Joan Wallach Scott's *Gender and the Politics of History*
Mary Wollstonecraft's *A Vindication of the Rights of Woman*
Virginia Woolf's *A Room of One's Own*

GEOGRAPHY

The Brundtland Report's *Our Common Future*
Rachel Carson's *Silent Spring*
Charles Darwin's *On the Origin of Species*
James Ferguson's *The Anti-Politics Machine*
Jane Jacobs's *The Death and Life of Great American Cities*
James Lovelock's *Gaia: A New Look at Life on Earth*
Amartya Sen's *Development as Freedom*
Mathis Wackernagel & William Rees's *Our Ecological Footprint*

HISTORY

Janet Abu-Lughod's *Before European Hegemony*
Benedict Anderson's *Imagined Communities*
Bernard Bailyn's *The Ideological Origins of the American Revolution*
Hanna Batatu's *The Old Social Classes And The Revolutionary Movements Of Iraq*
Christopher Browning's *Ordinary Men: Reserve Police Batallion 101 and the Final Solution in Poland*
Edmund Burke's *Reflections on the Revolution in France*
William Cronon's *Nature's Metropolis: Chicago And The Great West*
Alfred W. Crosby's *The Columbian Exchange*
Hamid Dabashi's *Iran: A People Interrupted*
David Brion Davis's *The Problem of Slavery in the Age of Revolution*
Nathalie Zemon Davis's *The Return of Martin Guerre*
Jared Diamond's *Guns, Germs & Steel: the Fate of Human Societies*
Frank Dikotter's *Mao's Great Famine*
John W Dower's *War Without Mercy: Race And Power In The Pacific War*
W. E. B. Du Bois's *The Souls of Black Folk*
Richard J. Evans's *In Defence of History*
Lucien Febvre's *The Problem of Unbelief in the 16th Century*
Sheila Fitzpatrick's *Everyday Stalinism*

Eric Foner's *Reconstruction: America's Unfinished Revolution, 1863-1877*
Michel Foucault's *Discipline and Punish*
Michel Foucault's *History of Sexuality*
Francis Fukuyama's *The End of History and the Last Man*
John Lewis Gaddis's *We Now Know: Rethinking Cold War History*
Ernest Gellner's *Nations and Nationalism*
Eugene Genovese's *Roll, Jordan, Roll: The World the Slaves Made*
Carlo Ginzburg's *The Night Battles*
Daniel Goldhagen's *Hitler's Willing Executioners*
Jack Goldstone's *Revolution and Rebellion in the Early Modern World*
Antonio Gramsci's *The Prison Notebooks*
Alexander Hamilton, John Jay & James Madison's *The Federalist Papers*
Christopher Hill's *The World Turned Upside Down*
Carole Hillenbrand's *The Crusades: Islamic Perspectives*
Thomas Hobbes's *Leviathan*
Eric Hobsbawm's *The Age Of Revolution*
John A. Hobson's *Imperialism: A Study*
Albert Hourani's *History of the Arab Peoples*
Samuel P. Huntington's *The Clash of Civilizations and the Remaking of World Order*
C. L. R. James's *The Black Jacobins*
Tony Judt's *Postwar: A History of Europe Since 1945*
Ernst Kantorowicz's *The King's Two Bodies: A Study in Medieval Political Theology*
Paul Kennedy's *The Rise and Fall of the Great Powers*
Ian Kershaw's *The "Hitler Myth": Image and Reality in the Third Reich*
John Maynard Keynes's *The General Theory of Employment, Interest and Money*
Charles P. Kindleberger's *Manias, Panics and Crashes*
Martin Luther King Jr's *Why We Can't Wait*
Henry Kissinger's *World Order: Reflections on the Character of Nations and the Course of History*
Thomas Kuhn's *The Structure of Scientific Revolutions*
Georges Lefebvre's *The Coming of the French Revolution*
John Locke's *Two Treatises of Government*
Niccolò Machiavelli's *The Prince*
Thomas Robert Malthus's *An Essay on the Principle of Population*
Mahmood Mamdani's *Citizen and Subject: Contemporary Africa And The Legacy Of Late Colonialism*
Karl Marx's *Capital*
Stanley Milgram's *Obedience to Authority*
John Stuart Mill's *On Liberty*
Thomas Paine's *Common Sense*
Thomas Paine's *Rights of Man*
Geoffrey Parker's *Global Crisis: War, Climate Change and Catastrophe in the Seventeenth Century*
Jonathan Riley-Smith's *The First Crusade and the Idea of Crusading*
Jean-Jacques Rousseau's *The Social Contract*
Joan Wallach Scott's *Gender and the Politics of History*
Theda Skocpol's *States and Social Revolutions*
Adam Smith's *The Wealth of Nations*
Timothy Snyder's *Bloodlands: Europe Between Hitler and Stalin*
Sun Tzu's *The Art of War*
Keith Thomas's *Religion and the Decline of Magic*
Thucydides's *The History of the Peloponnesian War*
Frederick Jackson Turner's *The Significance of the Frontier in American History*
Odd Arne Westad's *The Global Cold War: Third World Interventions And The Making Of Our Times*

LITERATURE

Chinua Achebe's *An Image of Africa: Racism in Conrad's Heart of Darkness*
Roland Barthes's *Mythologies*
Homi K. Bhabha's *The Location of Culture*
Judith Butler's *Gender Trouble*
Simone De Beauvoir's *The Second Sex*
Ferdinand De Saussure's *Course in General Linguistics*
T. S. Eliot's *The Sacred Wood: Essays on Poetry and Criticism*
Zora Neale Huston's *Characteristics of Negro Expression*
Toni Morrison's *Playing in the Dark: Whiteness in the American Literary Imagination*
Edward Said's *Orientalism*
Gayatri Chakravorty Spivak's *Can the Subaltern Speak?*
Mary Wollstonecraft's *A Vindication of the Rights of Women*
Virginia Woolf's *A Room of One's Own*

PHILOSOPHY

Elizabeth Anscombe's *Modern Moral Philosophy*
Hannah Arendt's *The Human Condition*
Aristotle's *Metaphysics*
Aristotle's *Nicomachean Ethics*
Edmund Gettier's *Is Justified True Belief Knowledge?*
Georg Wilhelm Friedrich Hegel's *Phenomenology of Spirit*
David Hume's *Dialogues Concerning Natural Religion*
David Hume's *The Enquiry for Human Understanding*
Immanuel Kant's *Religion within the Boundaries of Mere Reason*
Immanuel Kant's *Critique of Pure Reason*
Søren Kierkegaard's *The Sickness Unto Death*
Søren Kierkegaard's *Fear and Trembling*
C. S. Lewis's *The Abolition of Man*
Alasdair MacIntyre's *After Virtue*
Marcus Aurelius's *Meditations*
Friedrich Nietzsche's *On the Genealogy of Morality*
Friedrich Nietzsche's *Beyond Good and Evil*
Plato's *Republic*
Plato's *Symposium*
Jean-Jacques Rousseau's *The Social Contract*
Gilbert Ryle's *The Concept of Mind*
Baruch Spinoza's *Ethics*
Sun Tzu's *The Art of War*
Ludwig Wittgenstein's *Philosophical Investigations*

POLITICS

Benedict Anderson's *Imagined Communities*
Aristotle's *Politics*
Bernard Bailyn's *The Ideological Origins of the American Revolution*
Edmund Burke's *Reflections on the Revolution in France*
John C. Calhoun's *A Disquisition on Government*
Ha-Joon Chang's *Kicking Away the Ladder*
Hamid Dabashi's *Iran: A People Interrupted*
Hamid Dabashi's *Theology of Discontent: The Ideological Foundation of the Islamic Revolution in Iran*
Robert Dahl's *Democracy and its Critics*
Robert Dahl's *Who Governs?*
David Brion Davis's *The Problem of Slavery in the Age of Revolution*

The Macat Library By Discipline

Alexis De Tocqueville's *Democracy in America*
James Ferguson's *The Anti-Politics Machine*
Frank Dikotter's *Mao's Great Famine*
Sheila Fitzpatrick's *Everyday Stalinism*
Eric Foner's *Reconstruction: America's Unfinished Revolution, 1863-1877*
Milton Friedman's *Capitalism and Freedom*
Francis Fukuyama's *The End of History and the Last Man*
John Lewis Gaddis's *We Now Know: Rethinking Cold War History*
Ernest Gellner's *Nations and Nationalism*
David Graeber's *Debt: the First 5000 Years*
Antonio Gramsci's *The Prison Notebooks*
Alexander Hamilton, John Jay & James Madison's *The Federalist Papers*
Friedrich Hayek's *The Road to Serfdom*
Christopher Hill's *The World Turned Upside Down*
Thomas Hobbes's *Leviathan*
John A. Hobson's *Imperialism: A Study*
Samuel P. Huntington's *The Clash of Civilizations and the Remaking of World Order*
Tony Judt's *Postwar: A History of Europe Since 1945*
David C. Kang's *China Rising: Peace, Power and Order in East Asia*
Paul Kennedy's *The Rise and Fall of Great Powers*
Robert Keohane's *After Hegemony*
Martin Luther King Jr.'s *Why We Can't Wait*
Henry Kissinger's *World Order: Reflections on the Character of Nations and the Course of History*
John Locke's *Two Treatises of Government*
Niccolò Machiavelli's *The Prince*
Thomas Robert Malthus's *An Essay on the Principle of Population*
Mahmood Mamdani's *Citizen and Subject: Contemporary Africa And The Legacy Of Late Colonialism*
Karl Marx's *Capital*
John Stuart Mill's *On Liberty*
John Stuart Mill's *Utilitarianism*
Hans Morgenthau's *Politics Among Nations*
Thomas Paine's *Common Sense*
Thomas Paine's *Rights of Man*
Thomas Piketty's *Capital in the Twenty-First Century*
Robert D. Putman's *Bowling Alone*
John Rawls's *Theory of Justice*
Jean-Jacques Rousseau's *The Social Contract*
Theda Skocpol's *States and Social Revolutions*
Adam Smith's *The Wealth of Nations*
Sun Tzu's *The Art of War*
Henry David Thoreau's *Civil Disobedience*
Thucydides's *The History of the Peloponnesian War*
Kenneth Waltz's *Theory of International Politics*
Max Weber's *Politics as a Vocation*
Odd Arne Westad's *The Global Cold War: Third World Interventions And The Making Of Our Times*

POSTCOLONIAL STUDIES

Roland Barthes's *Mythologies*
Frantz Fanon's *Black Skin, White Masks*
Homi K. Bhabha's *The Location of Culture*
Gustavo Gutiérrez's *A Theology of Liberation*
Edward Said's *Orientalism*
Gayatri Chakravorty Spivak's *Can the Subaltern Speak?*

PSYCHOLOGY

Gordon Allport's *The Nature of Prejudice*
Alan Baddeley & Graham Hitch's *Aggression: A Social Learning Analysis*
Albert Bandura's *Aggression: A Social Learning Analysis*
Leon Festinger's *A Theory of Cognitive Dissonance*
Sigmund Freud's *The Interpretation of Dreams*
Betty Friedan's *The Feminine Mystique*
Michael R. Gottfredson & Travis Hirschi's *A General Theory of Crime*
Eric Hoffer's *The True Believer: Thoughts on the Nature of Mass Movements*
William James's *Principles of Psychology*
Elizabeth Loftus's *Eyewitness Testimony*
A. H. Maslow's *A Theory of Human Motivation*
Stanley Milgram's *Obedience to Authority*
Steven Pinker's *The Better Angels of Our Nature*
Oliver Sacks's *The Man Who Mistook His Wife For a Hat*
Richard Thaler & Cass Sunstein's *Nudge: Improving Decisions About Health, Wealth and Happiness*
Amos Tversky's *Judgment under Uncertainty: Heuristics and Biases*
Philip Zimbardo's *The Lucifer Effect*

SCIENCE

Rachel Carson's *Silent Spring*
William Cronon's *Nature's Metropolis: Chicago And The Great West*
Alfred W. Crosby's *The Columbian Exchange*
Charles Darwin's *On the Origin of Species*
Richard Dawkins's *The Selfish Gene*
Thomas Kuhn's *The Structure of Scientific Revolutions*
Geoffrey Parker's *Global Crisis: War, Climate Change and Catastrophe in the Seventeenth Century*
Mathis Wackernagel & William Rees's *Our Ecological Footprint*

SOCIOLOGY

Michelle Alexander's *The New Jim Crow: Mass Incarceration in the Age of Colorblindness*
Gordon Allport's *The Nature of Prejudice*
Albert Bandura's *Aggression: A Social Learning Analysis*
Hanna Batatu's *The Old Social Classes And The Revolutionary Movements Of Iraq*
Ha-Joon Chang's *Kicking Away the Ladder*
W. E. B. Du Bois's *The Souls of Black Folk*
Émile Durkheim's *On Suicide*
Frantz Fanon's *Black Skin, White Masks*
Frantz Fanon's *The Wretched of the Earth*
Eric Foner's *Reconstruction: America's Unfinished Revolution, 1863-1877*
Eugene Genovese's *Roll, Jordan, Roll: The World the Slaves Made*
Jack Goldstone's *Revolution and Rebellion in the Early Modern World*
Antonio Gramsci's *The Prison Notebooks*
Richard Herrnstein & Charles A Murray's *The Bell Curve: Intelligence and Class Structure in American Life*
Eric Hoffer's *The True Believer: Thoughts on the Nature of Mass Movements*
Jane Jacobs's *The Death and Life of Great American Cities*
Robert Lucas's *Why Doesn't Capital Flow from Rich to Poor Countries?*
Jay Macleod's *Ain't No Makin' It: Aspirations and Attainment in a Low Income Neighborhood*
Elaine May's *Homeward Bound: American Families in the Cold War Era*
Douglas McGregor's *The Human Side of Enterprise*
C. Wright Mills's *The Sociological Imagination*

The Macat Library By Discipline

Thomas Piketty's *Capital in the Twenty-First Century*
Robert D. Putman's *Bowling Alone*
David Riesman's *The Lonely Crowd: A Study of the Changing American Character*
Edward Said's *Orientalism*
Joan Wallach Scott's *Gender and the Politics of History*
Theda Skocpol's *States and Social Revolutions*
Max Weber's *The Protestant Ethic and the Spirit of Capitalism*

THEOLOGY

Augustine's *Confessions*
Benedict's *Rule of St Benedict*
Gustavo Gutiérrez's *A Theology of Liberation*
Carole Hillenbrand's *The Crusades: Islamic Perspectives*
David Hume's *Dialogues Concerning Natural Religion*
Immanuel Kant's *Religion within the Boundaries of Mere Reason*
Ernst Kantorowicz's *The King's Two Bodies: A Study in Medieval Political Theology*
Søren Kierkegaard's *The Sickness Unto Death*
C. S. Lewis's *The Abolition of Man*
Saba Mahmood's *The Politics of Piety: The Islamic Revival and the Feminist Subject*
Baruch Spinoza's *Ethics*
Keith Thomas's *Religion and the Decline of Magic*

COMING SOON

Chris Argyris's *The Individual and the Organisation*
Seyla Benhabib's *The Rights of Others*
Walter Benjamin's *The Work Of Art in the Age of Mechanical Reproduction*
John Berger's *Ways of Seeing*
Pierre Bourdieu's *Outline of a Theory of Practice*
Mary Douglas's *Purity and Danger*
Roland Dworkin's *Taking Rights Seriously*
James G. March's *Exploration and Exploitation in Organisational Learning*
Ikujiro Nonaka's *A Dynamic Theory of Organizational Knowledge Creation*
Griselda Pollock's *Vision and Difference*
Amartya Sen's *Inequality Re-Examined*
Susan Sontag's *On Photography*
Yasser Tabbaa's *The Transformation of Islamic Art*
Ludwig von Mises's *Theory of Money and Credit*

Macat Disciplines

Access the greatest ideas and thinkers across entire disciplines, including

GLOBALIZATION

Arjun Appadurai's, *Modernity at Large: Cultural Dimensions of Globalisation*

James Ferguson's, *The Anti-Politics Machine*

Geert Hofstede's, *Culture's Consequences*

Amartya Sen's, *Development as Freedom*

Macat analyses are available from all good bookshops and libraries.

Access hundreds of analyses through one, multimedia tool.
Join free for one month **library.macat.com**

Macat Disciplines

Access the greatest ideas and thinkers across entire disciplines, including

MAN AND THE ENVIRONMENT

 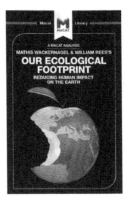

The Brundtland Report's, *Our Common Future*
Rachel Carson's, *Silent Spring*
James Lovelock's, *Gaia: A New Look at Life on Earth*
Mathis Wackernagel & William Rees's, *Our Ecological Footprint*

Macat analyses are available from all good bookshops and libraries.

Access hundreds of analyses through one, multimedia tool.
Join free for one month **library.macat.com**

Macat Disciplines

Access the greatest ideas and thinkers across entire disciplines, including

THE FUTURE OF DEMOCRACY

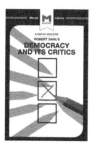   

Robert A. Dahl's, *Democracy and Its Critics*
Robert A. Dahl's, *Who Governs?*
Alexis De Toqueville's, *Democracy in America*
Niccolò Machiavelli's, *The Prince*
John Stuart Mill's, *On Liberty*
Robert D. Putnam's, *Bowling Alone*
Jean-Jacques Rousseau's, *The Social Contract*
Henry David Thoreau's, *Civil Disobedience*

Macat analyses are available from all good bookshops and libraries.

Access hundreds of analyses through one, multimedia tool.
Join free for one month **library.macat.com**

Macat Disciplines

Access the greatest ideas and thinkers across entire disciplines, including

TOTALITARIANISM

Sheila Fitzpatrick's, *Everyday Stalinism*
Ian Kershaw's, *The "Hitler Myth"*
Timothy Snyder's, *Bloodlands*

Macat Pairs

*Analyse historical and modern issues
from opposite sides of an argument.
Pairs include:*

RACE AND IDENTITY

Zora Neale Hurston's
Characteristics of Negro Expression

Using material collected on anthropological
expeditions to the South, Zora Neale Hurston explains
how expression in African American culture in the
early twentieth century departs from the art of white
America. At the time, African American art was often
criticized for copying white culture. For Hurston, this
criticism misunderstood how art works. European
tradition views art as something fixed. But Hurston
describes a creative process that is alive, ever-
changing, and largely improvisational. She maintains
that African American art works through a process
called 'mimicry'—where an imitated object or verbal
pattern, for example, is reshaped and altered until
it becomes something new, novel—and worthy of
attention.

Frantz Fanon's
Black Skin, White Masks

Black Skin, White Masks offers a radical analysis of the
psychological effects of colonization on the colonized.

Fanon witnessed the effects of colonization first
hand both in his birthplace, Martinique, and again
later in life when he worked as a psychiatrist
in another French colony, Algeria. His text is
uncompromising in form and argument. He
dissects the dehumanizing effects of colonialism,
arguing that it destroys the native sense of identity,
forcing people to adapt to an alien set of values—
including a core belief that they are inferior. This
results in deep psychological trauma.

Fanon's work played a pivotal role in the civil rights
movements of the 1960s.

Macat analyses are available from all good bookshops and libraries.

Access hundreds of analyses through one, multimedia tool.
Join free for one month **library.macat.com**

Macat Pairs

Analyse historical and modern issues from opposite sides of an argument. Pairs include:

INTERNATIONAL RELATIONS IN THE 21ST CENTURY

Samuel P. Huntington's
The Clash of Civilisations

In his highly influential 1996 book, Huntington offers a vision of a post-Cold War world in which conflict takes place not between competing ideologies but between cultures. The worst clash, he argues, will be between the Islamic world and the West: the West's arrogance and belief that its culture is a "gift" to the world will come into conflict with Islam's obstinacy and concern that its culture is under attack from a morally decadent "other."

Clash inspired much debate between different political schools of thought. But its greatest impact came in helping define American foreign policy in the wake of the 2001 terrorist attacks in New York and Washington.

Francis Fukuyama's
The End of History and the Last Man

Published in 1992, *The End of History and the Last Man* argues that capitalist democracy is the final destination for all societies. Fukuyama believed democracy triumphed during the Cold War because it lacks the "fundamental contradictions" inherent in communism and satisfies our yearning for freedom and equality. Democracy therefore marks the endpoint in the evolution of ideology, and so the "end of history." There will still be "events," but no fundamental change in ideology.

Macat Pairs

Analyse historical and modern issues from opposite sides of an argument. Pairs include:

HOW TO RUN AN ECONOMY

John Maynard Keynes's
The General Theory OF Employment, Interest and Money

Classical economics suggests that market economies are self-correcting in times of recession or depression, and tend toward full employment and output. But English economist John Maynard Keynes disagrees.

In his ground-breaking 1936 study *The General Theory*, Keynes argues that traditional economics has misunderstood the causes of unemployment. Employment is not determined by the price of labor; it is directly linked to demand. Keynes believes market economies are by nature unstable, and so require government intervention. Spurred on by the social catastrophe of the Great Depression of the 1930s, he sets out to revolutionize the way the world thinks

Milton Friedman's
The Role of Monetary Policy

Friedman's 1968 paper changed the course of economic theory. In just 17 pages, he demolished existing theory and outlined an effective alternate monetary policy designed to secure 'high employment, stable prices and rapid growth.'

Friedman demonstrated that monetary policy plays a vital role in broader economic stability and argued that economists got their monetary policy wrong in the 1950s and 1960s by misunderstanding the relationship between inflation and unemployment. Previous generations of economists had believed that governments could permanently decrease unemployment by permitting inflation—and vice versa. Friedman's most original contribution was to show that this supposed trade-off is an illusion that only works in the short term.

Macat analyses are available from all good bookshops and libraries.

Access hundreds of analyses through one, multimedia tool.
Join free for one month **library.macat.com**

Macat Pairs

Analyse historical and modern issues from opposite sides of an argument. Pairs include:

ARE WE FUNDAMENTALLY GOOD - OR BAD?

Steven Pinker's
The Better Angels of Our Nature

Stephen Pinker's gloriously optimistic 2011 book argues that, despite humanity's biological tendency toward violence, we are, in fact, less violent today than ever before. To prove his case, Pinker lays out pages of detailed statistical evidence. For him, much of the credit for the decline goes to the eighteenth-century Enlightenment movement, whose ideas of liberty, tolerance, and respect for the value of human life filtered down through society and affected how people thought. That psychological change led to behavioral change—and overall we became more peaceful. Critics countered that humanity could never overcome the biological urge toward violence; others argued that Pinker's statistics were flawed.

Philip Zimbardo's
The Lucifer Effect

Some psychologists believe those who commit cruelty are innately evil. Zimbardo disagrees. In *The Lucifer Effect*, he argues that sometimes good people do evil things simply because of the situations they find themselves in, citing many historical examples to illustrate his point. Zimbardo details his 1971 Stanford prison experiment, where ordinary volunteers playing guards in a mock prison rapidly became abusive. But he also describes the tortures committed by US army personnel in Iraq's Abu Ghraib prison in 2003—and how he himself testified in defence of one of those guards. committed by US army personnel in Iraq's Abu Ghraib prison in 2003—and how he himself testified in defence of one of those guards.

Macat analyses are available from all good bookshops and libraries.

Access hundreds of analyses through one, multimedia tool.
Join free for one month **library.macat.com**

Macat Pairs

Analyse historical and modern issues from opposite sides of an argument. Pairs include:

HOW WE RELATE TO EACH OTHER AND SOCIETY

Jean-Jacques Rousseau's
The Social Contract

Rousseau's famous work sets out the radical concept of the 'social contract': a give-and-take relationship between individual freedom and social order.

If people are free to do as they like, governed only by their own sense of justice, they are also vulnerable to chaos and violence. To avoid this, Rousseau proposes, they should agree to give up some freedom to benefit from the protection of social and political organization. But this deal is only just if societies are led by the collective needs and desires of the people, and able to control the private interests of individuals. For Rousseau, the only legitimate form of government is rule by the people.

Robert D. Putnam's
Bowling Alone

In *Bowling Alone*, Robert Putnam argues that Americans have become disconnected from one another and from the institutions of their common life, and investigates the consequences of this change.

Looking at a range of indicators, from membership in formal organizations to the number of invitations being extended to informal dinner parties, Putnam demonstrates that Americans are interacting less and creating less "social capital" – with potentially disastrous implications for their society.

It would be difficult to overstate the impact of *Bowling Alone*, one of the most frequently cited social science publications of the last half-century.

Macat analyses are available from all good bookshops and libraries.

Access hundreds of analyses through one, multimedia tool.
Join free for one month **library.macat.com**

For Product Safety Concerns and Information please contact our EU
representative GPSR@taylorandfrancis.com Taylor & Francis Verlag GmbH,
Kaufingerstraße 24, 80331 München, Germany

Printed and bound by CPI Group (UK) Ltd, Croydon, CR0 4YY
08/06/2025
01896977-0010